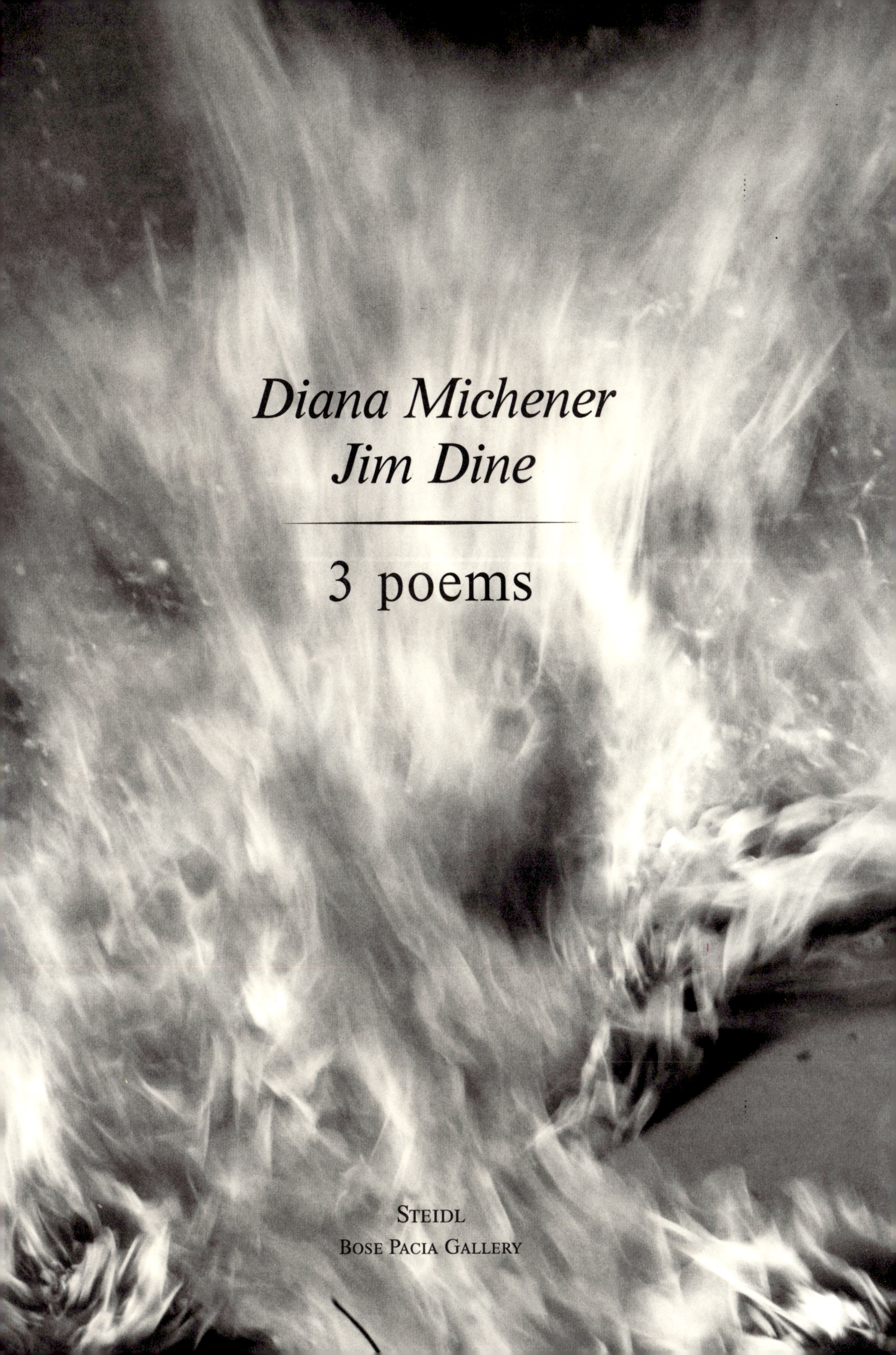

Diana Michener
Jim Dine

---

3 poems

STEIDL
BOSE PACIA GALLERY

Technicolor rose　　my toes are red　　the woodpe

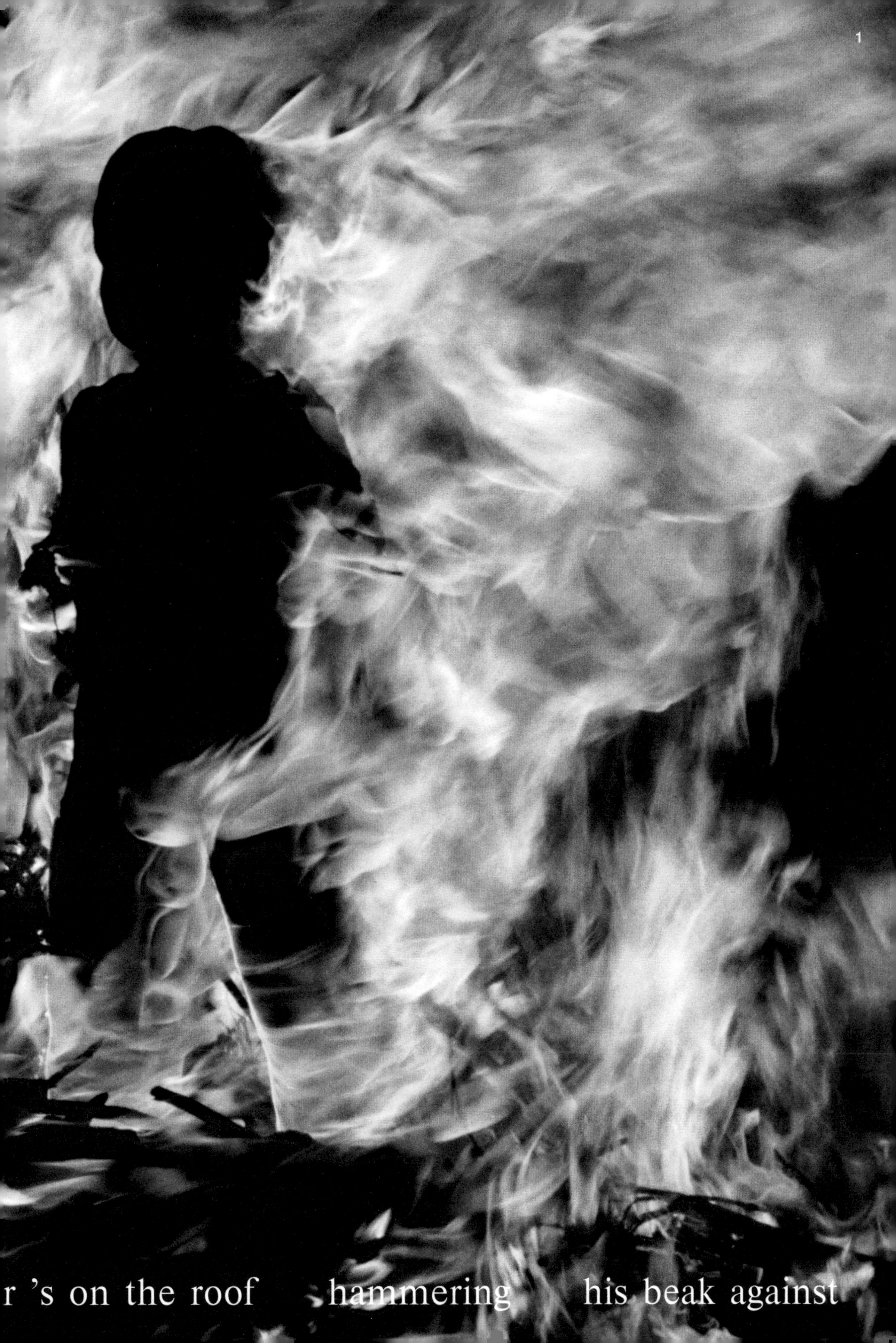

r 's on the roof hammering his beak against

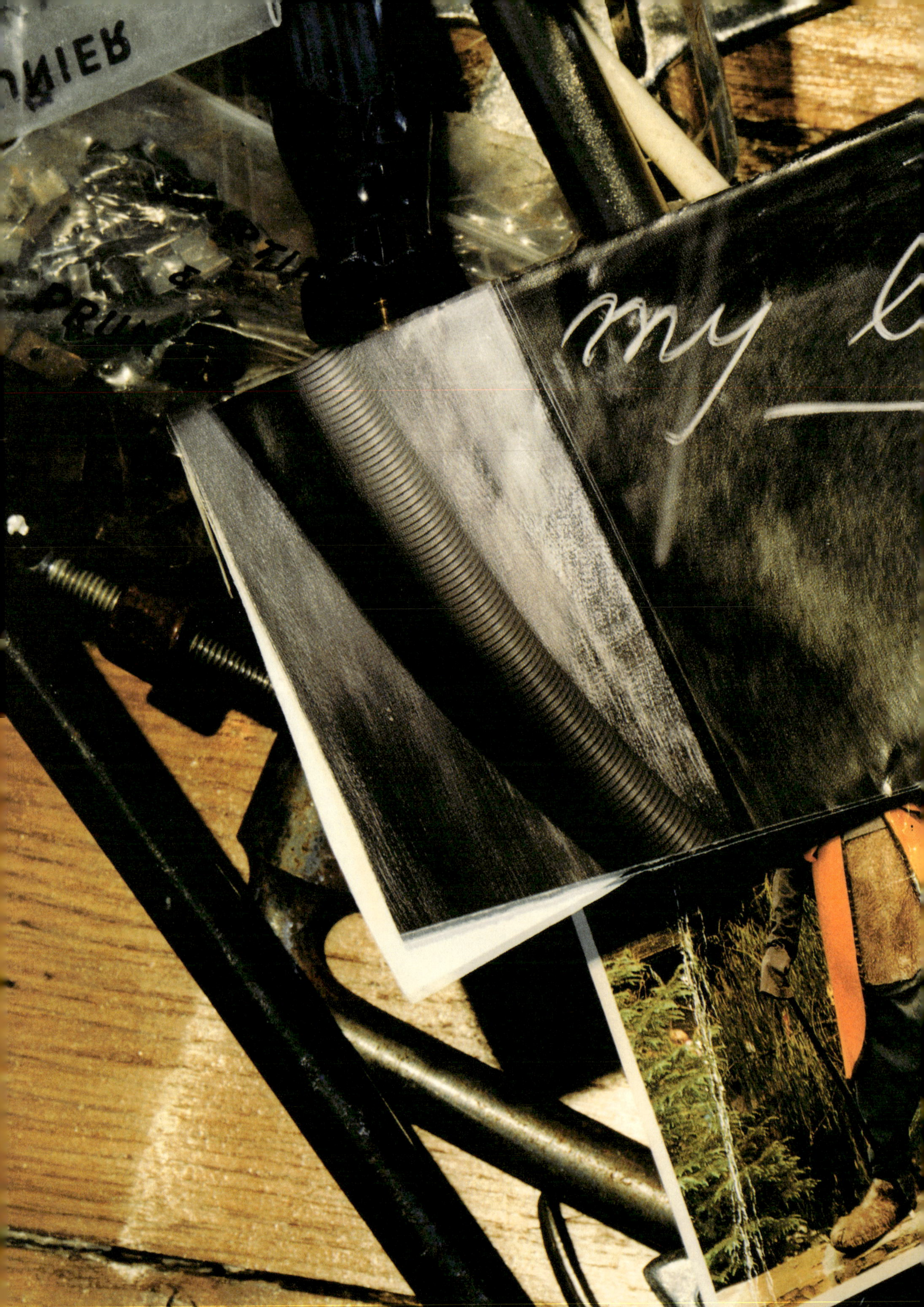

Pliers climbs the post he was sent and we

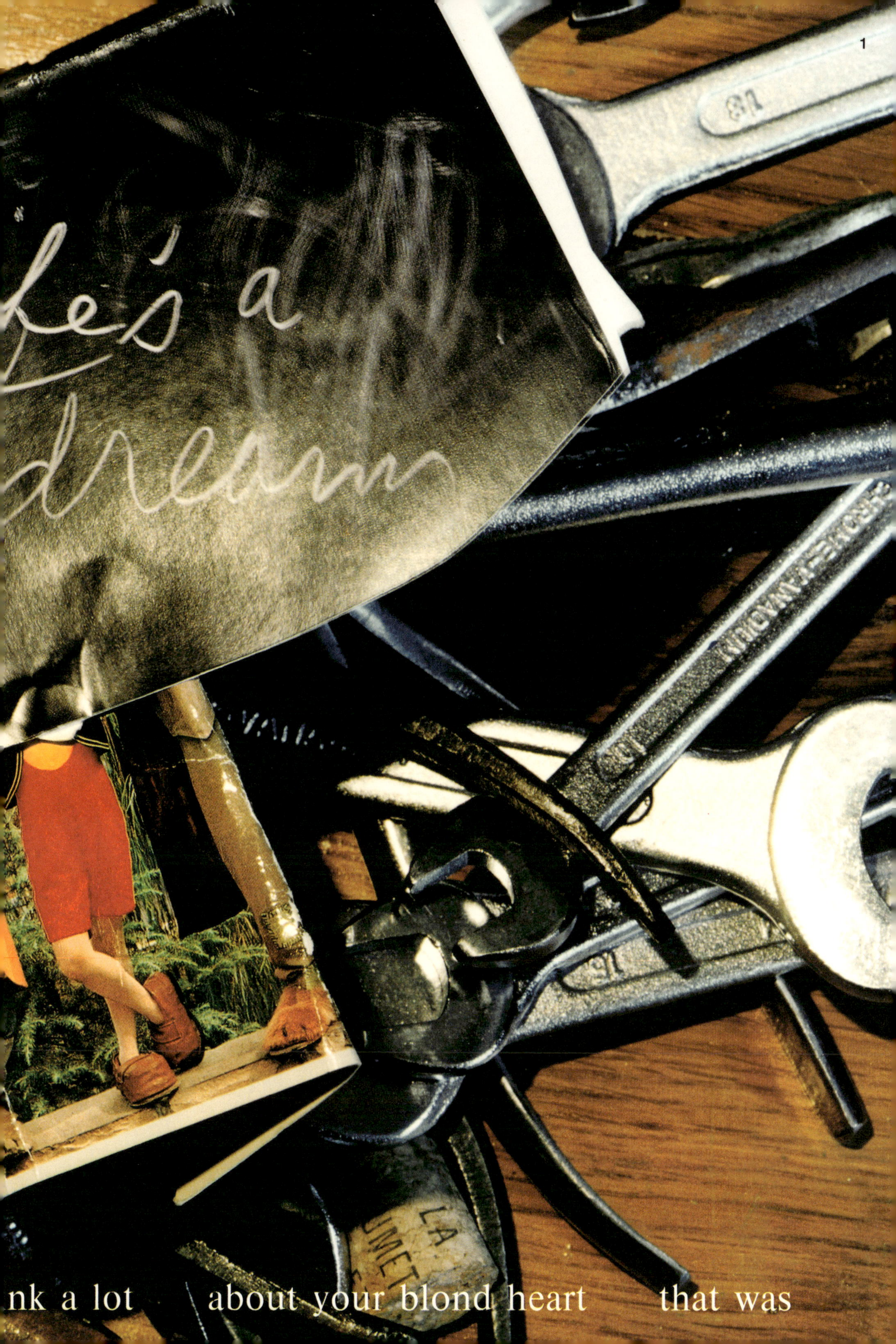

nk a lot about your blond heart that was

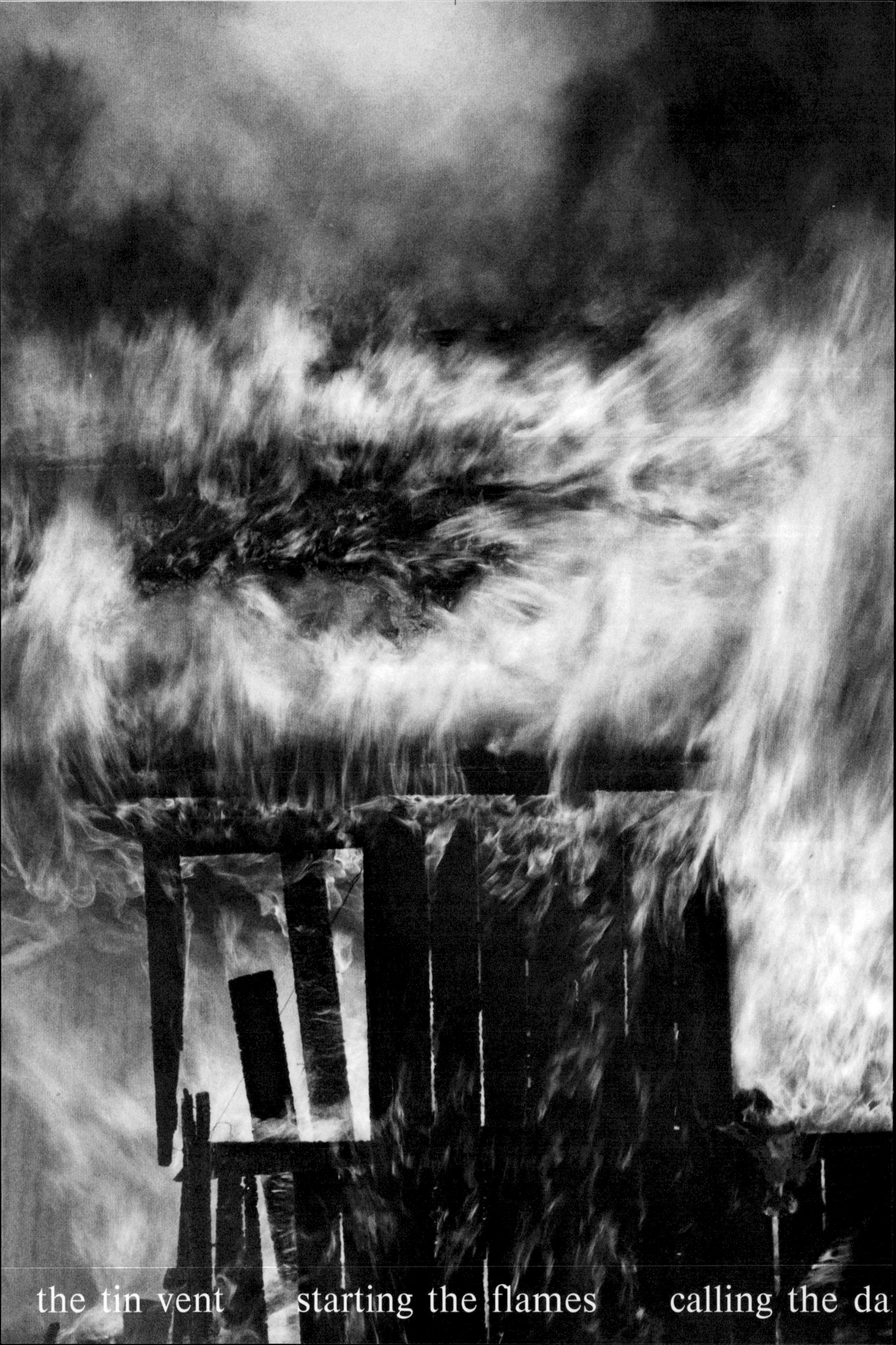

the tin vent   starting the flames   calling the da

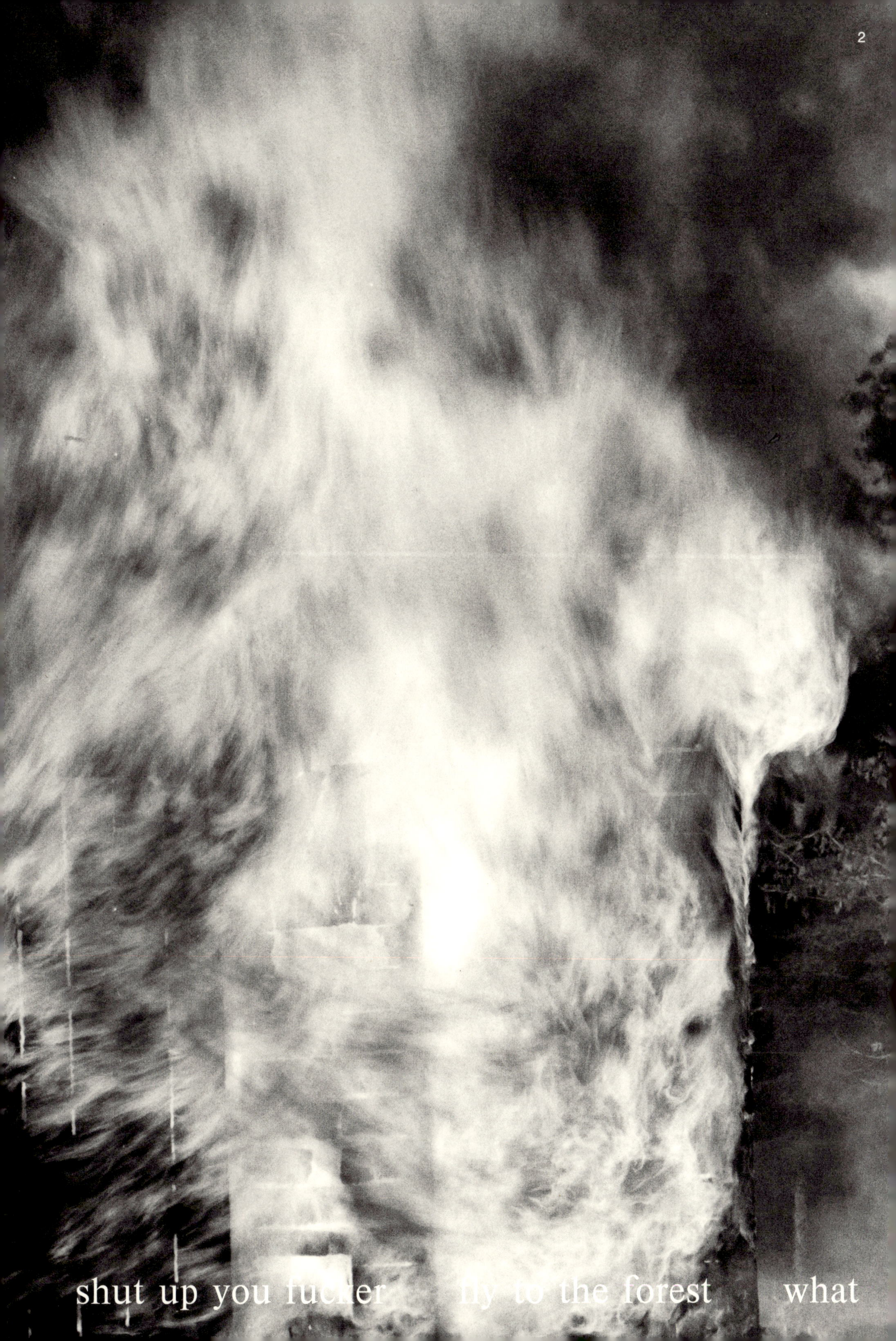
shut up you fucker fly to the forest what

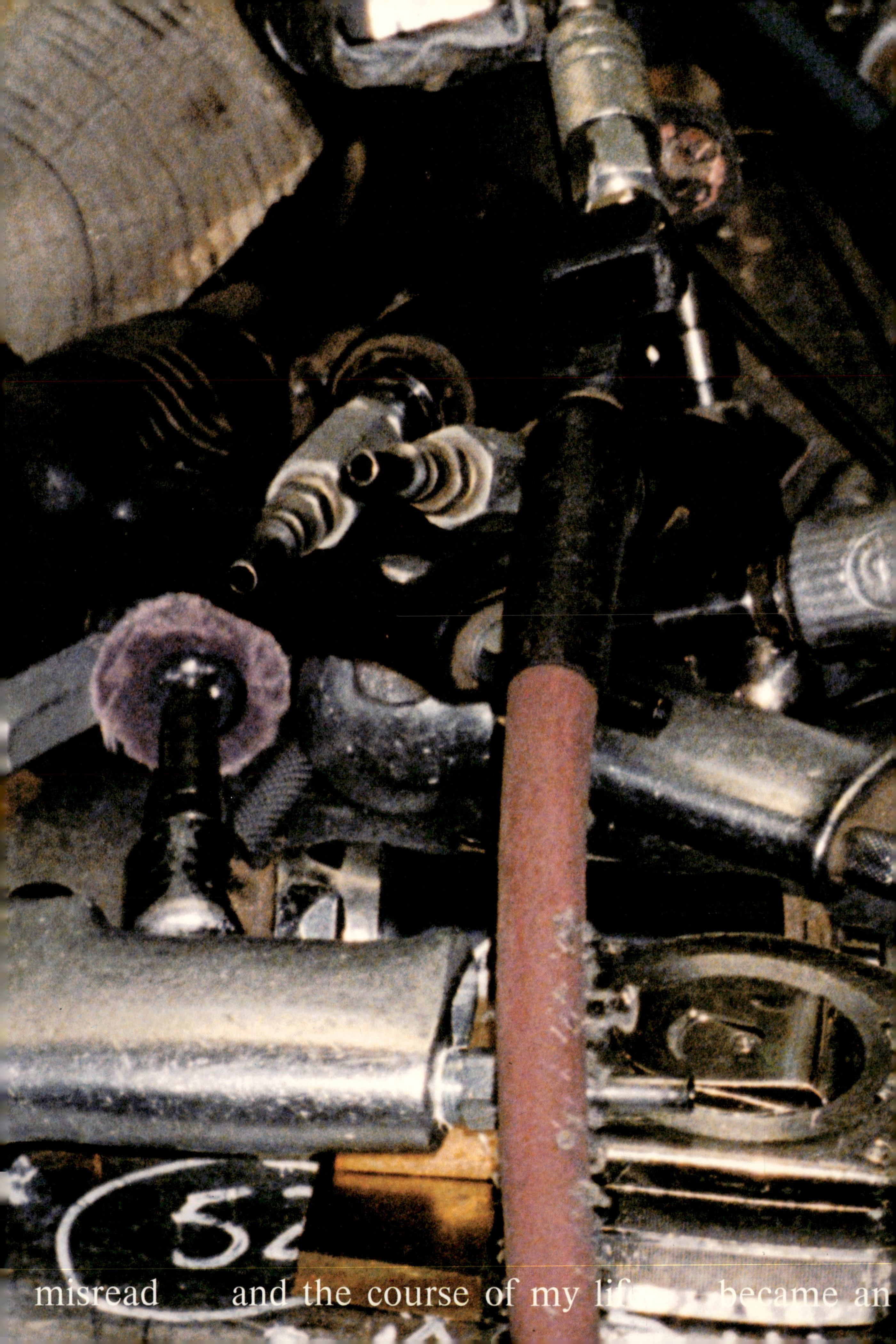

misread and the course of my life became an

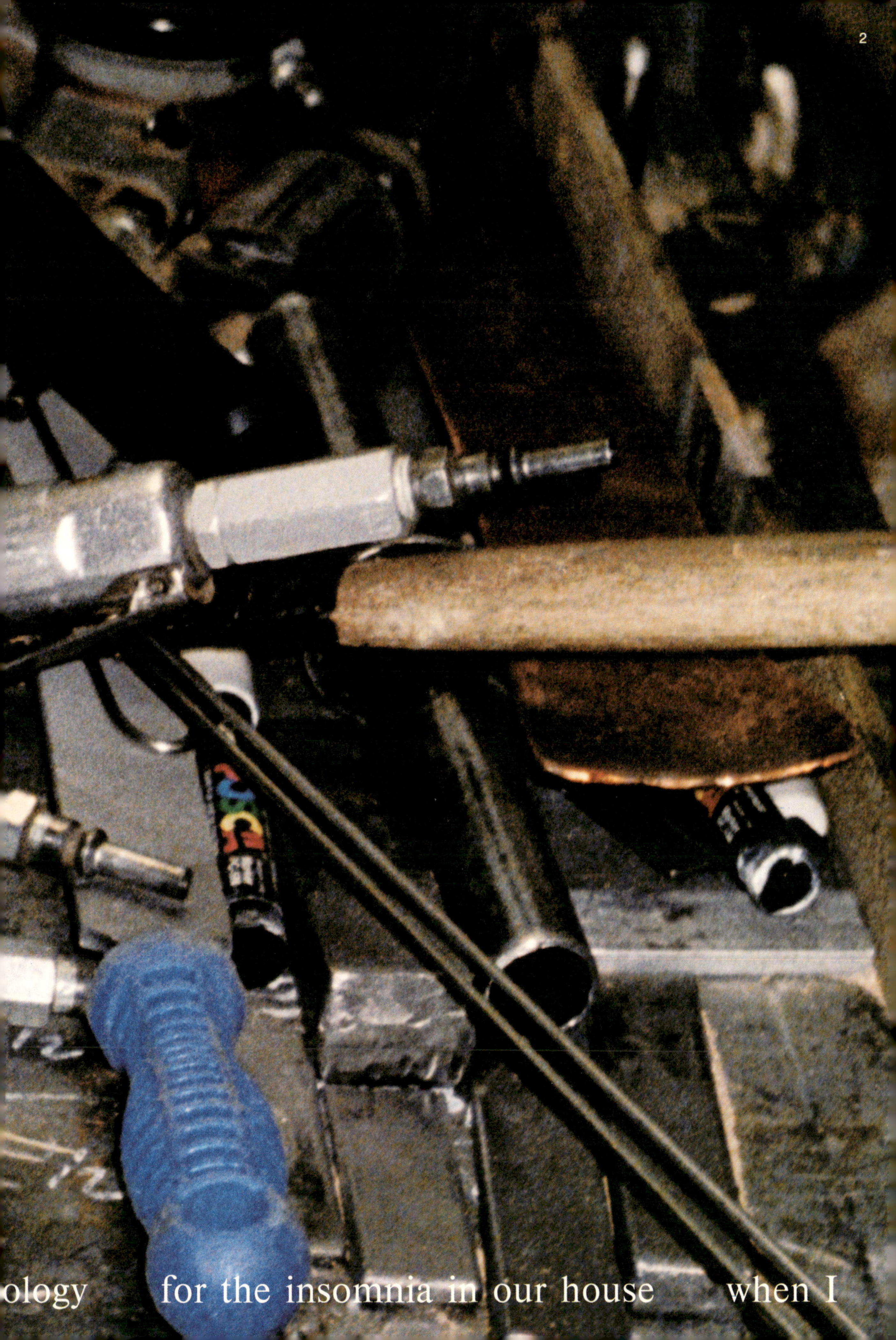

ology for the insomnia in our house when I

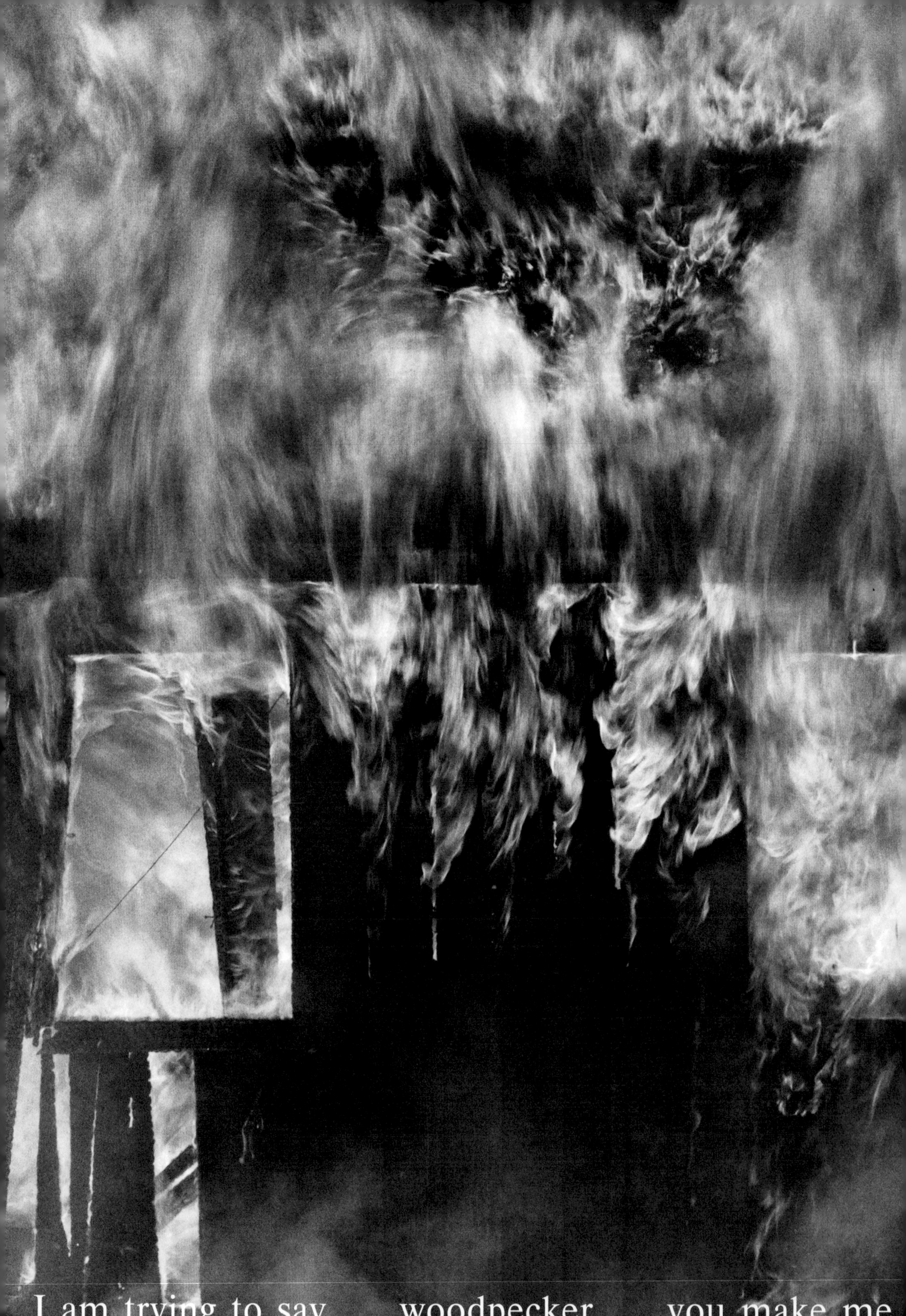

I am trying to say woodpecker you make me

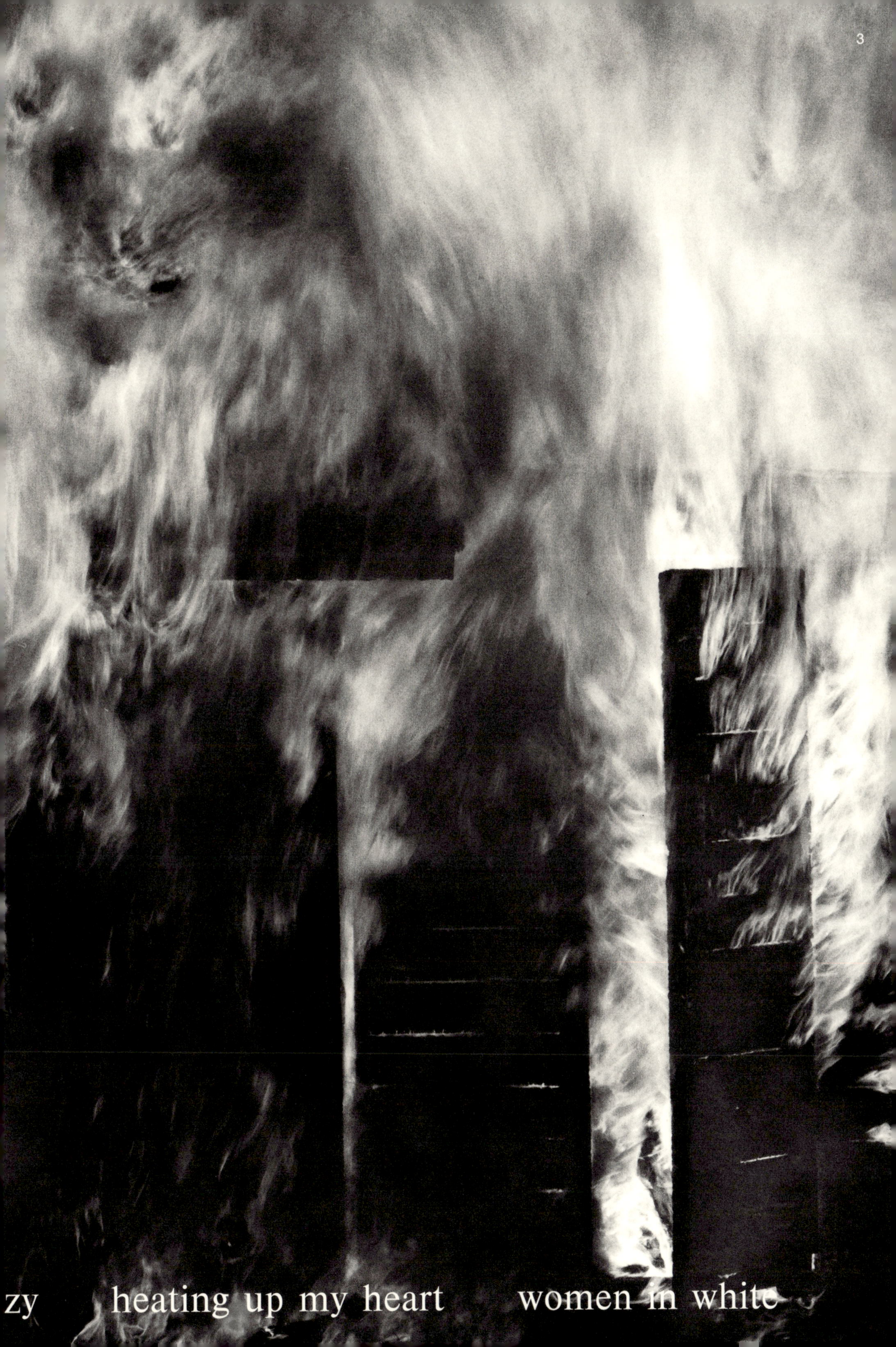
zy
heating up my heart
women in white

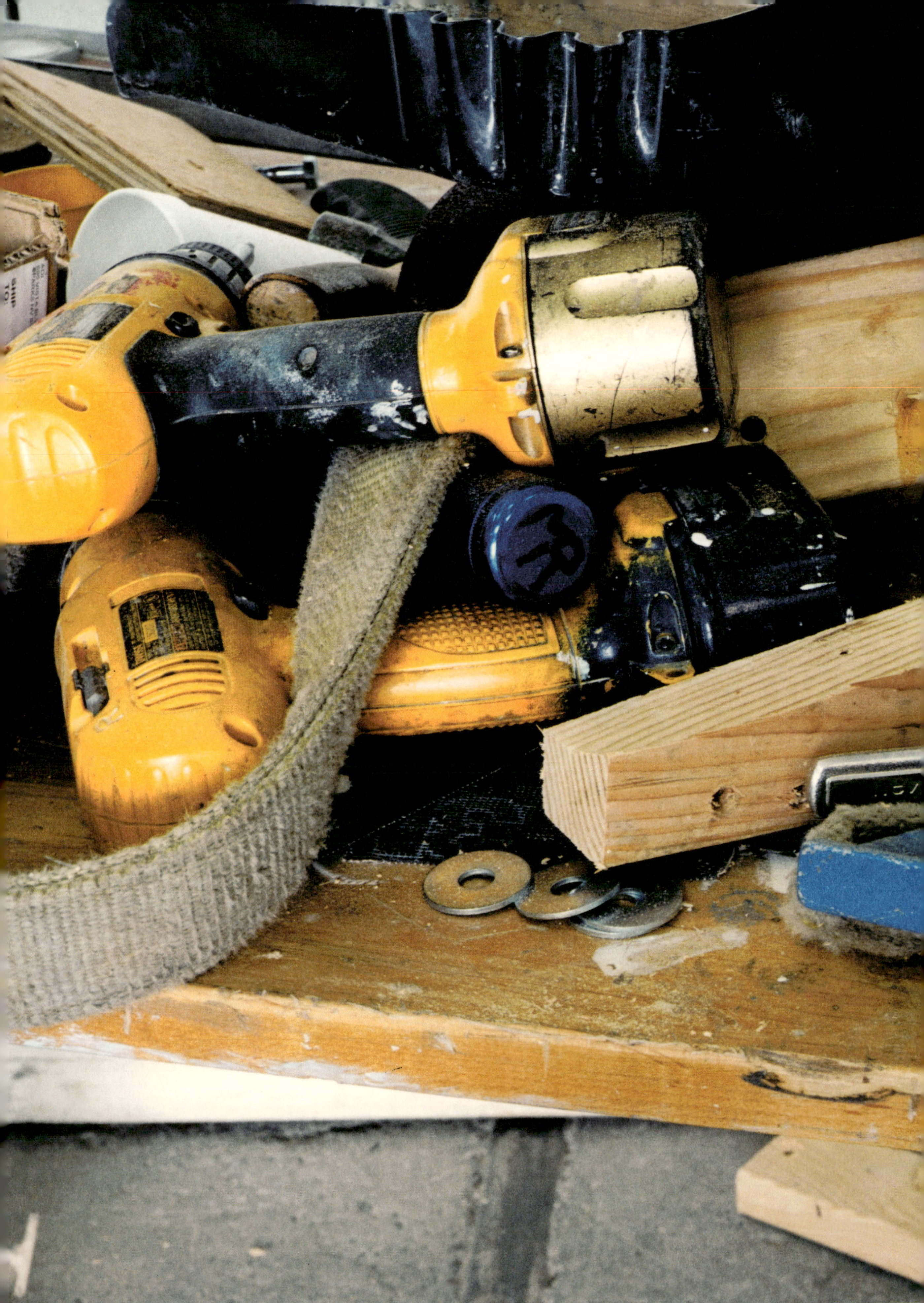

see the dancers tutus hanging side by side at the

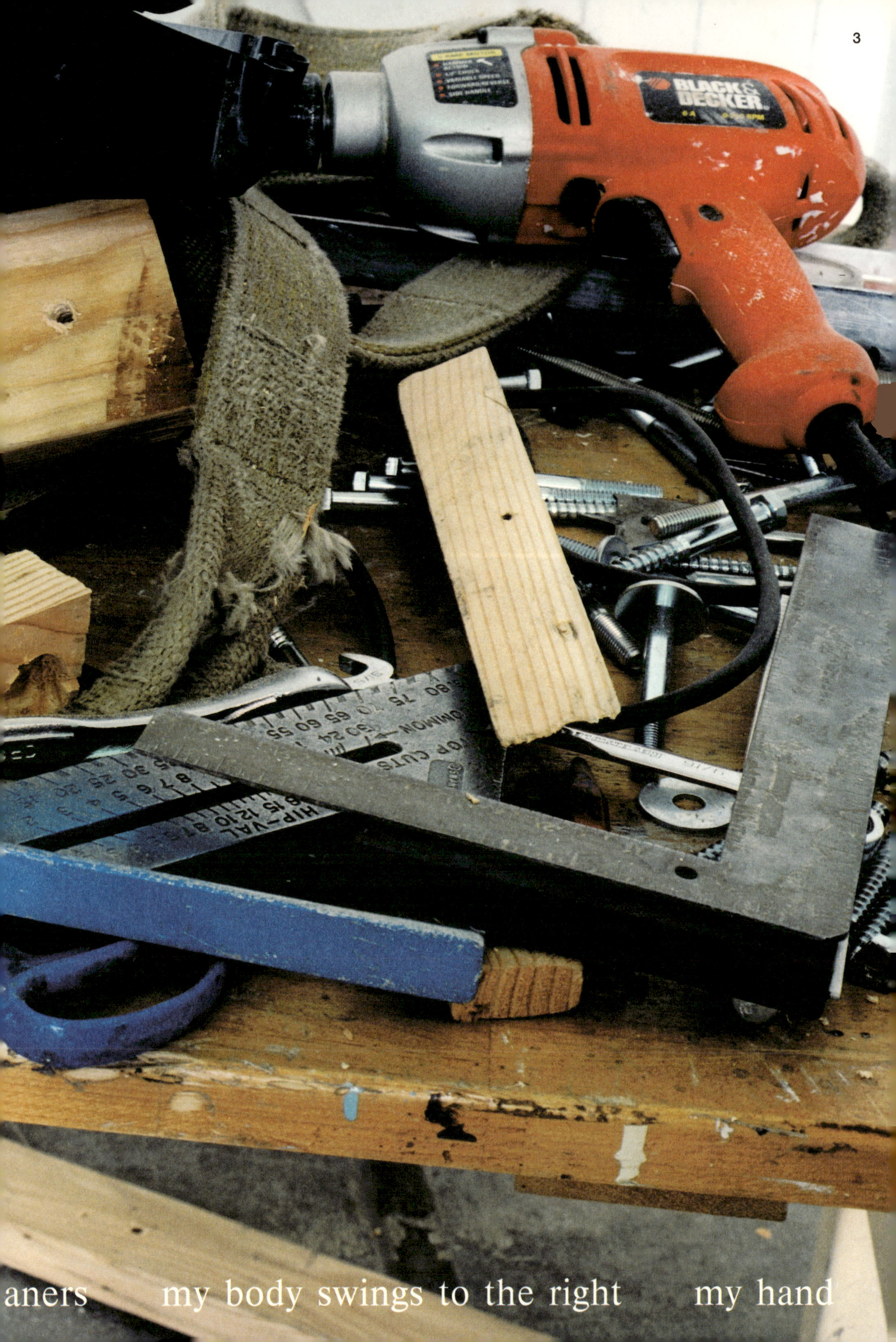

aners my body swings to the right my hand

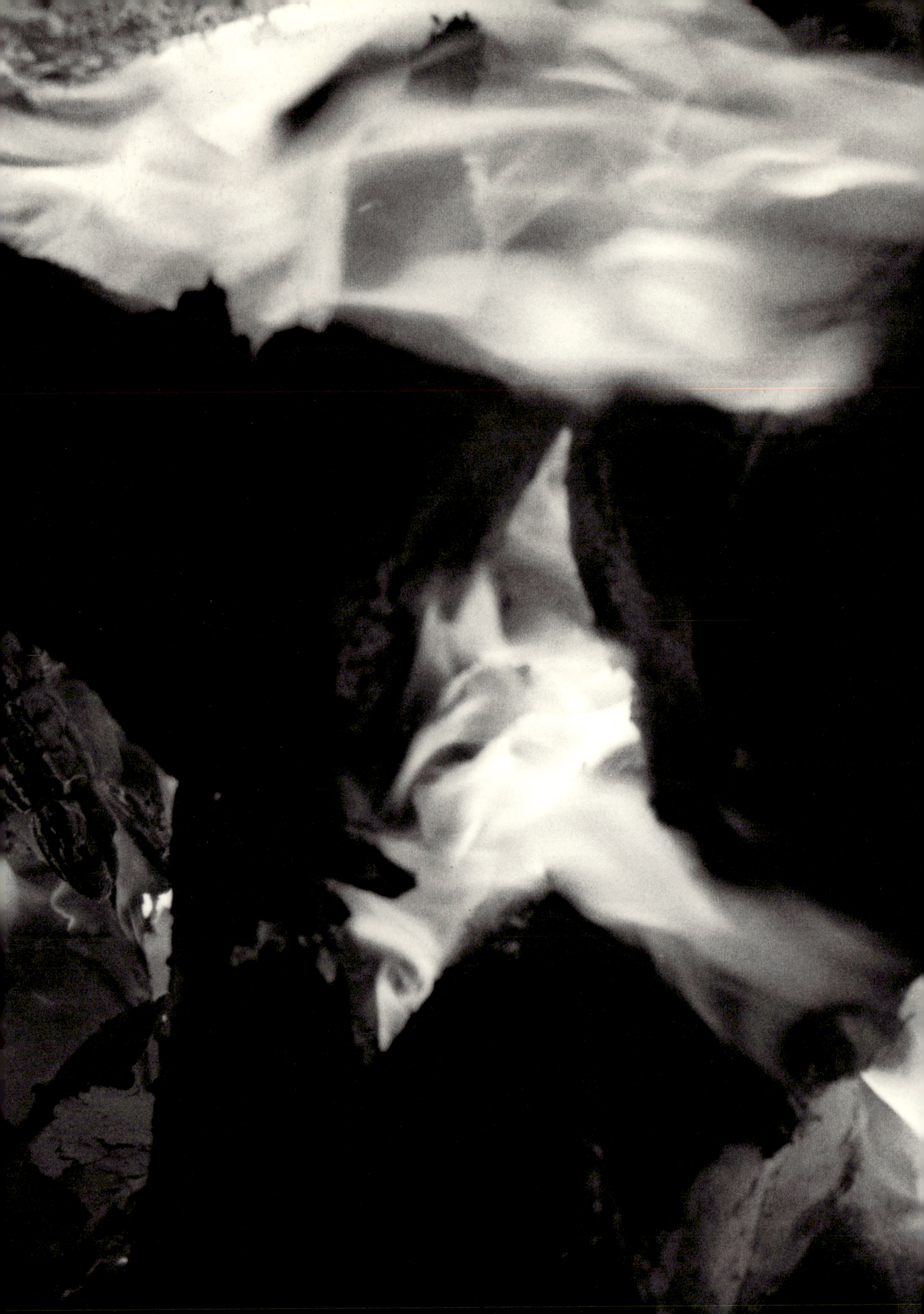

nightgowns run to the county jail help me he

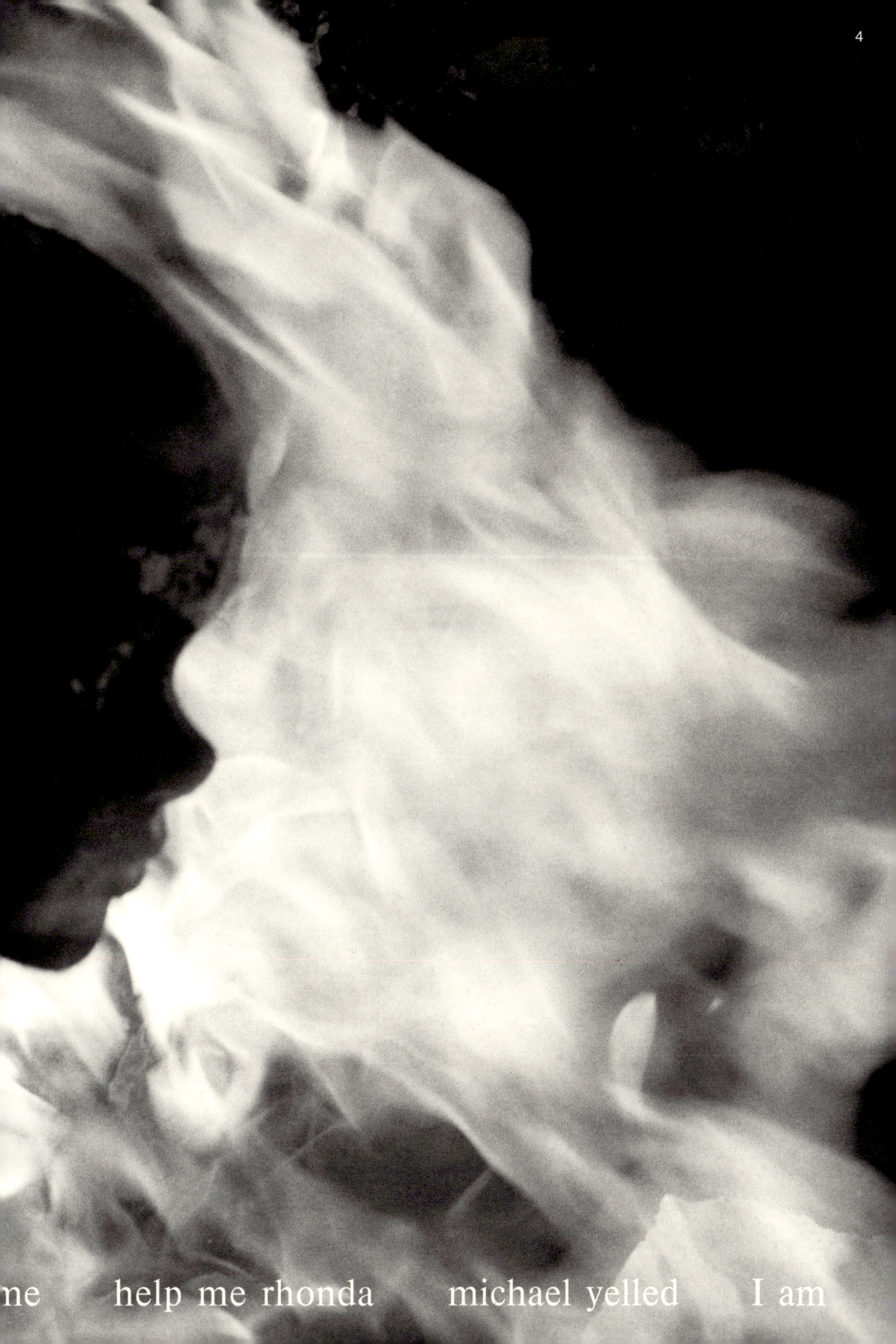
me help me rhonda michael yelled I am

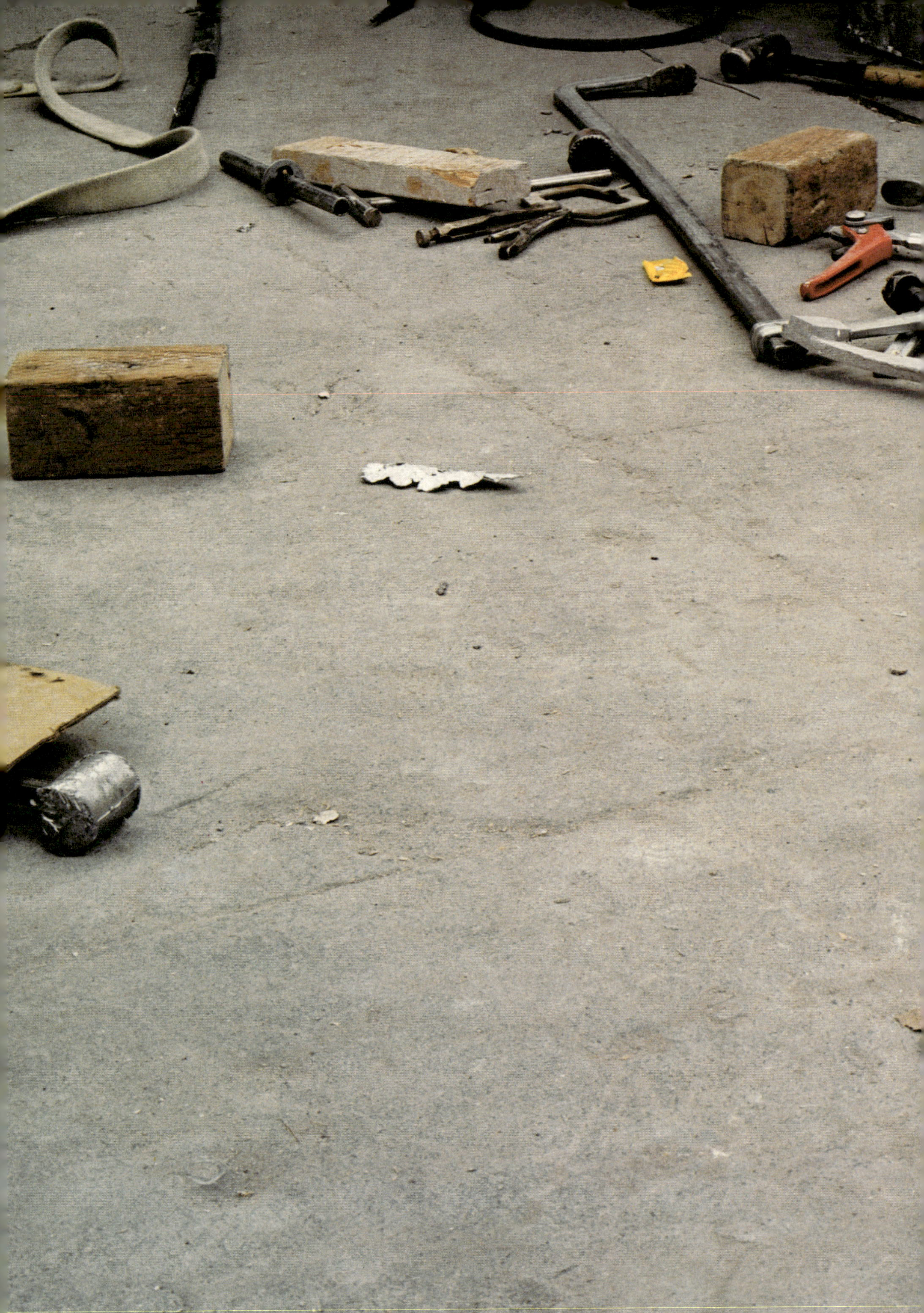

as usual mixes various grey tones and your n

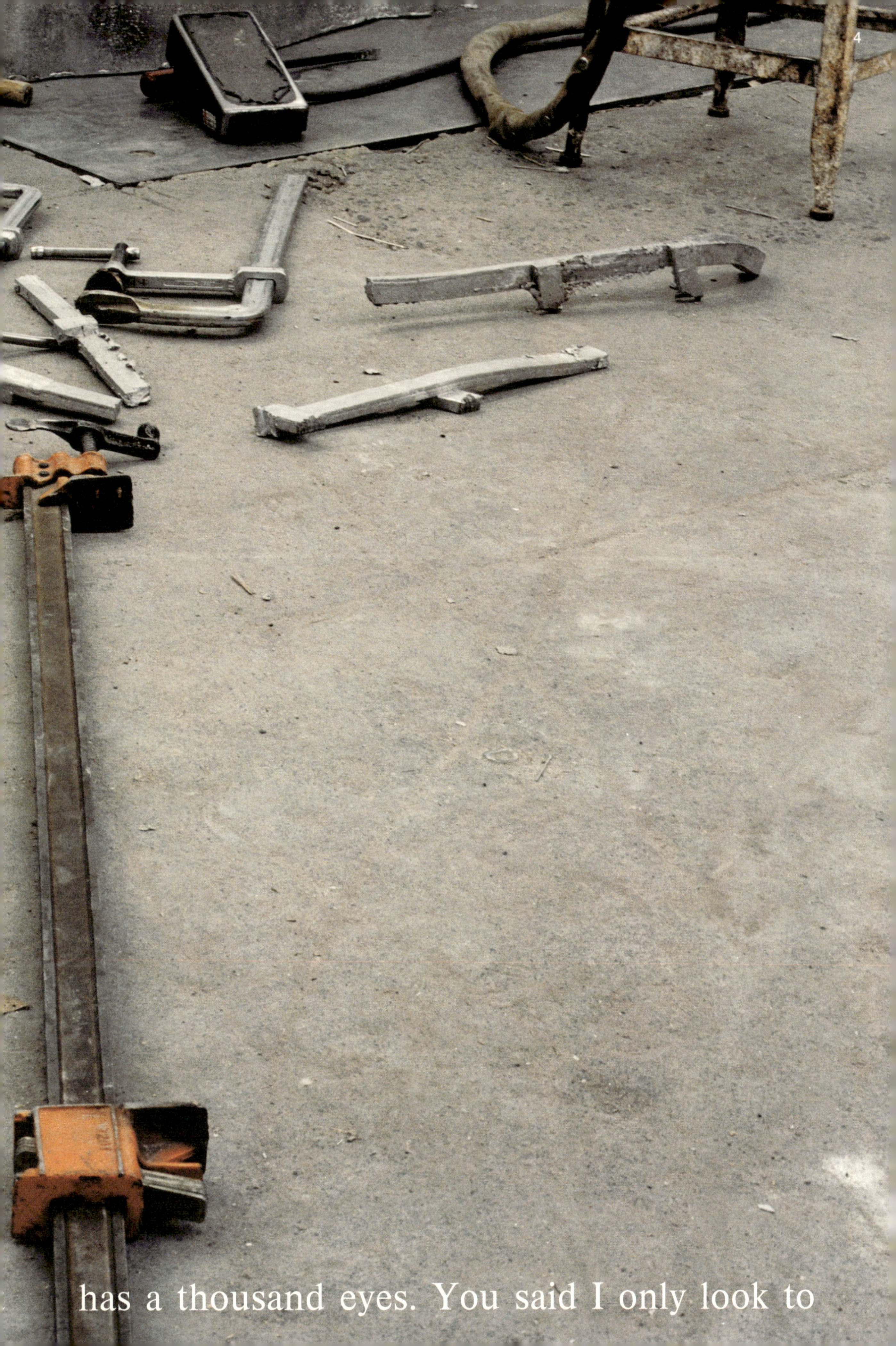

has a thousand eyes. You said I only look to

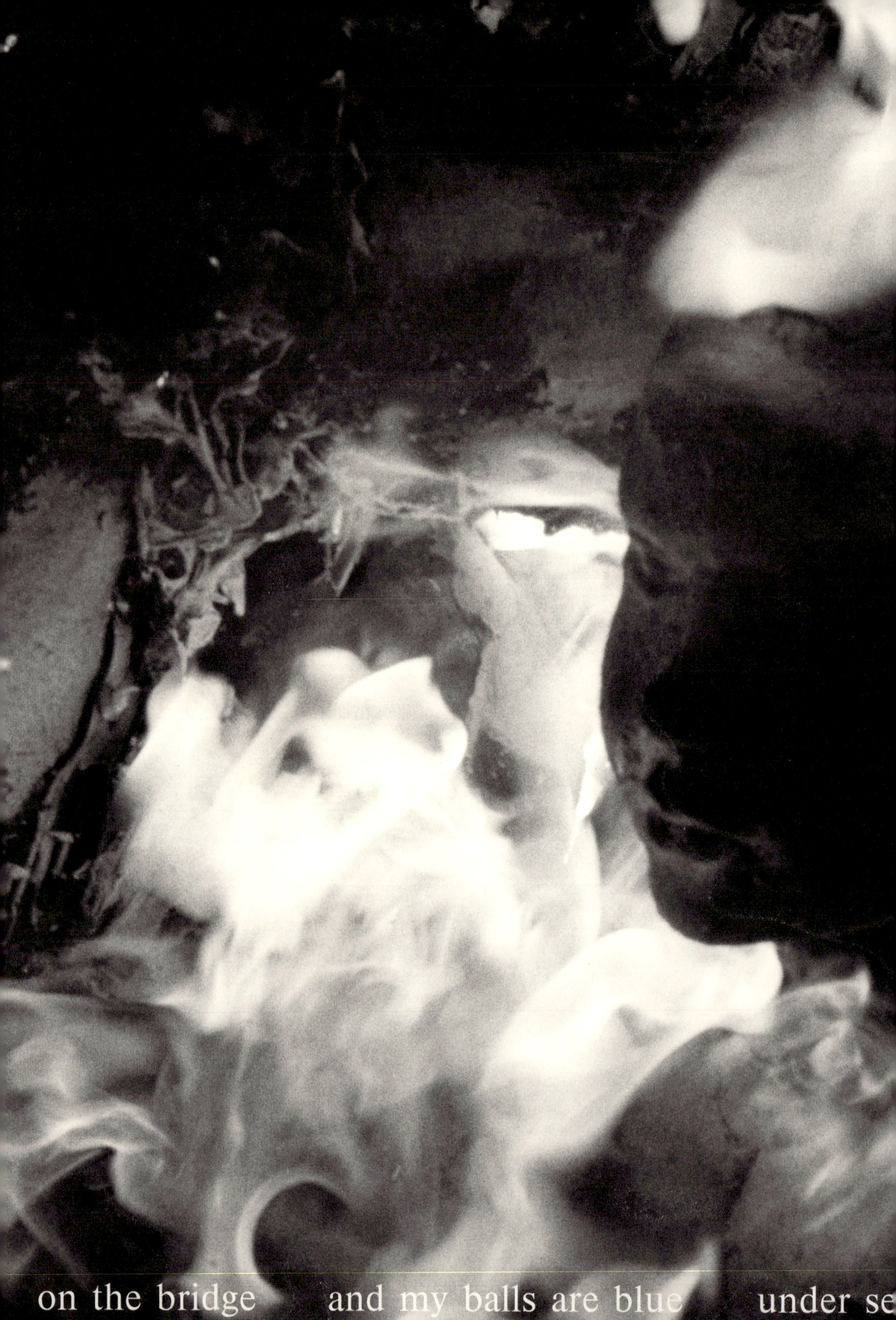

on the bridge and my balls are blue under se

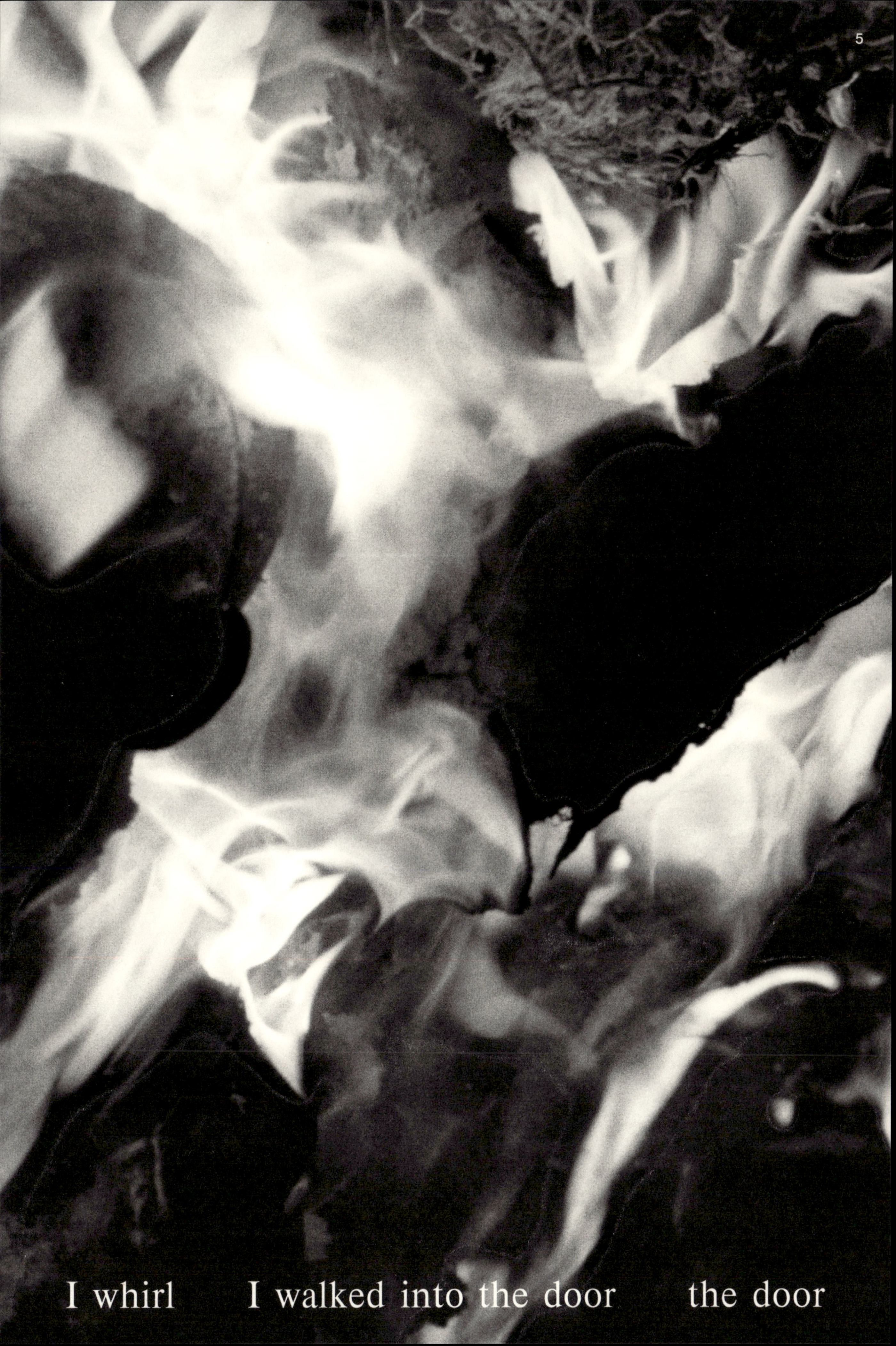

I whirl I walked into the door the door

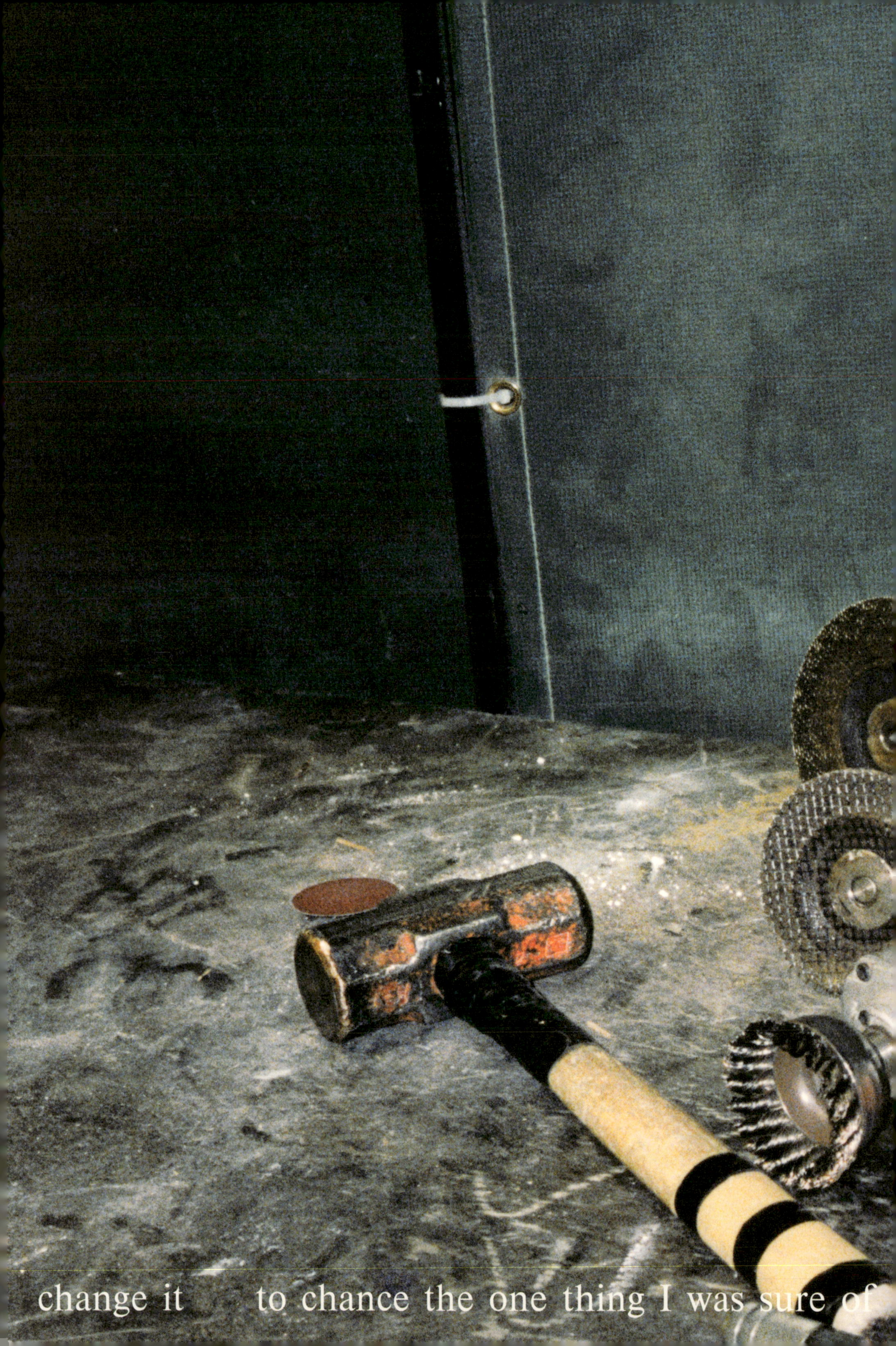

change it to chance the one thing I was sure of

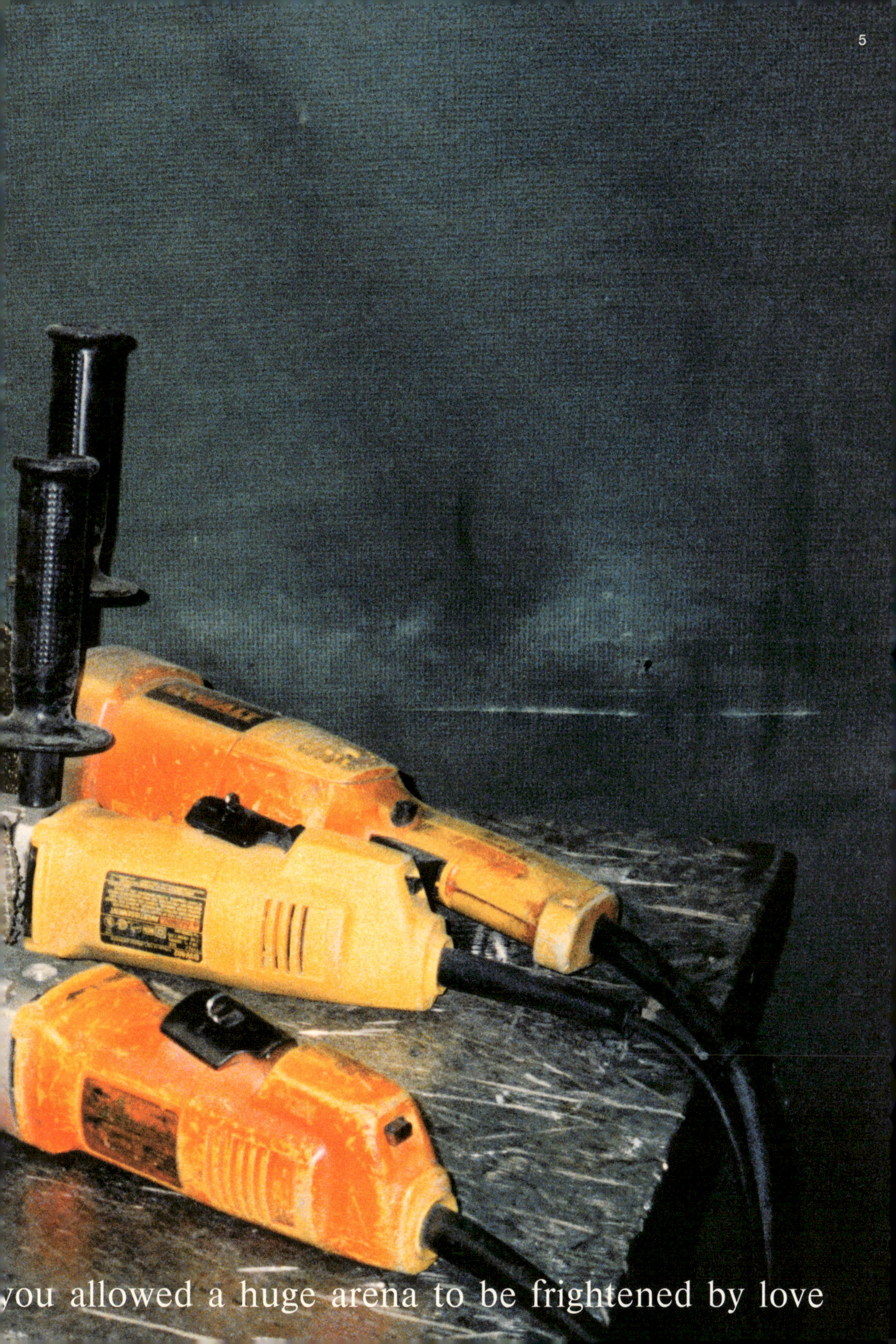

you allowed a huge arena to be frightened by love

opened I asked is you or me here we mis

s I said my mother died I laugh everyday

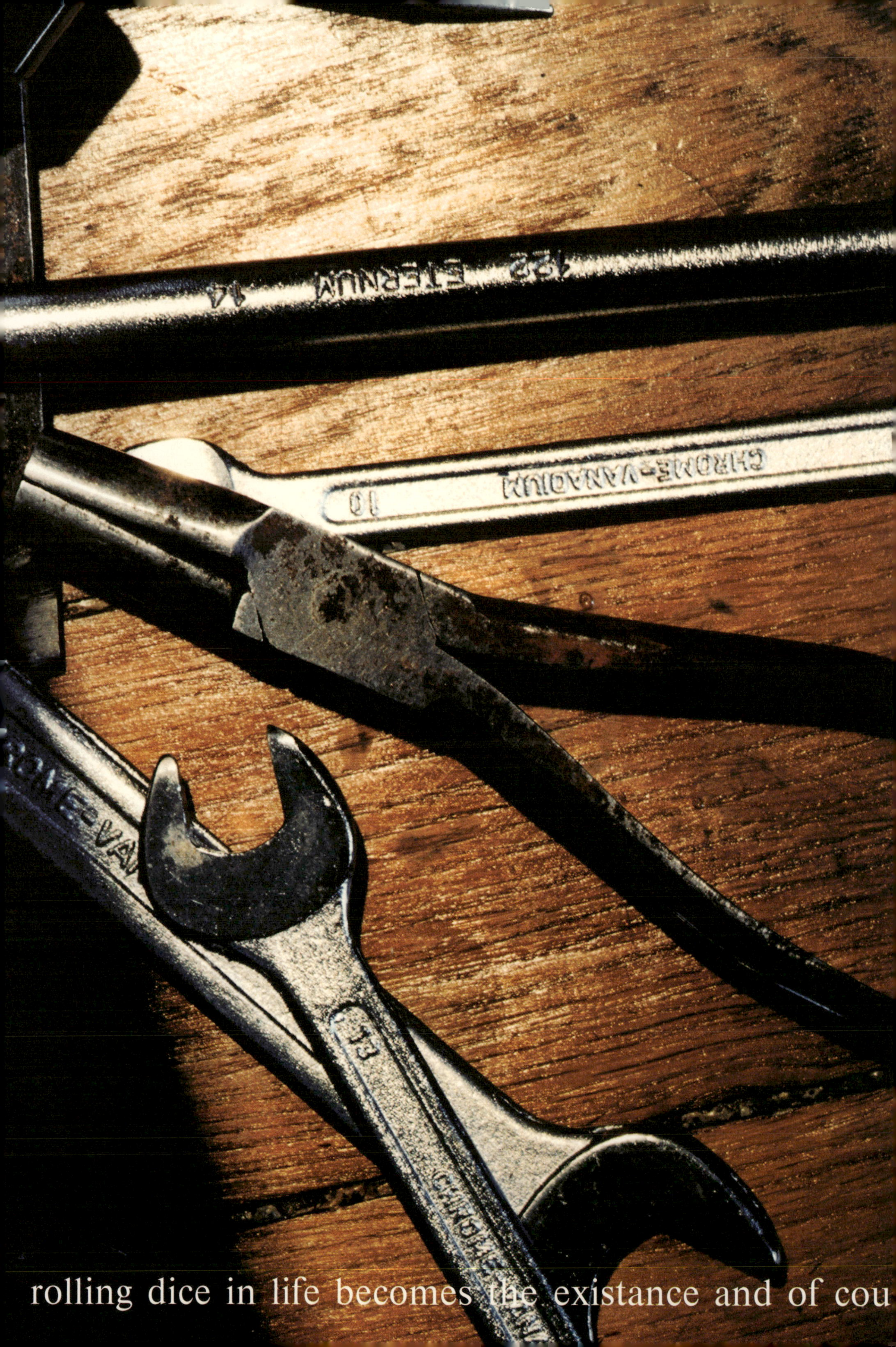

rolling dice in life becomes the existance and of cou

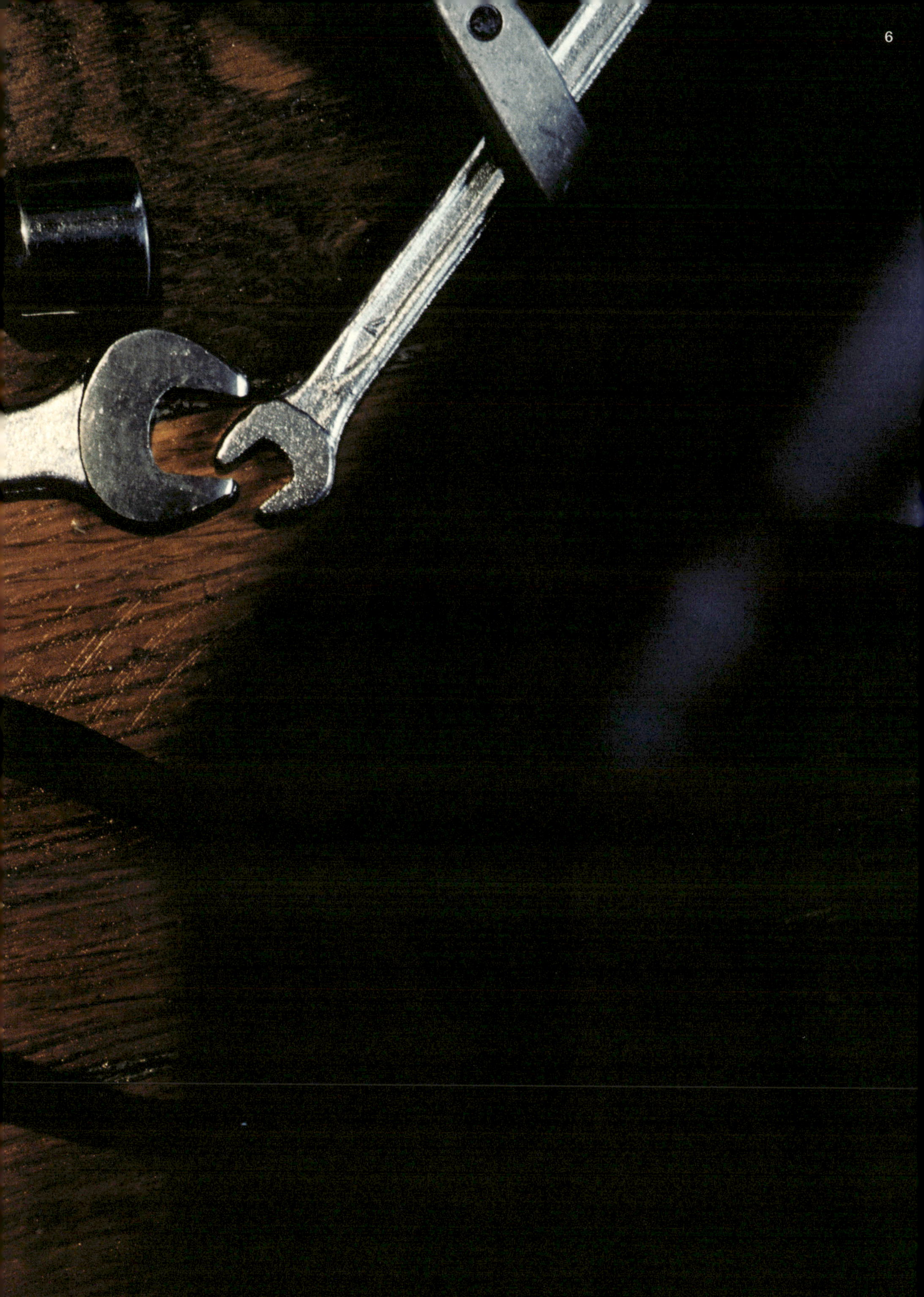

the fact that the saboteur crept into the house

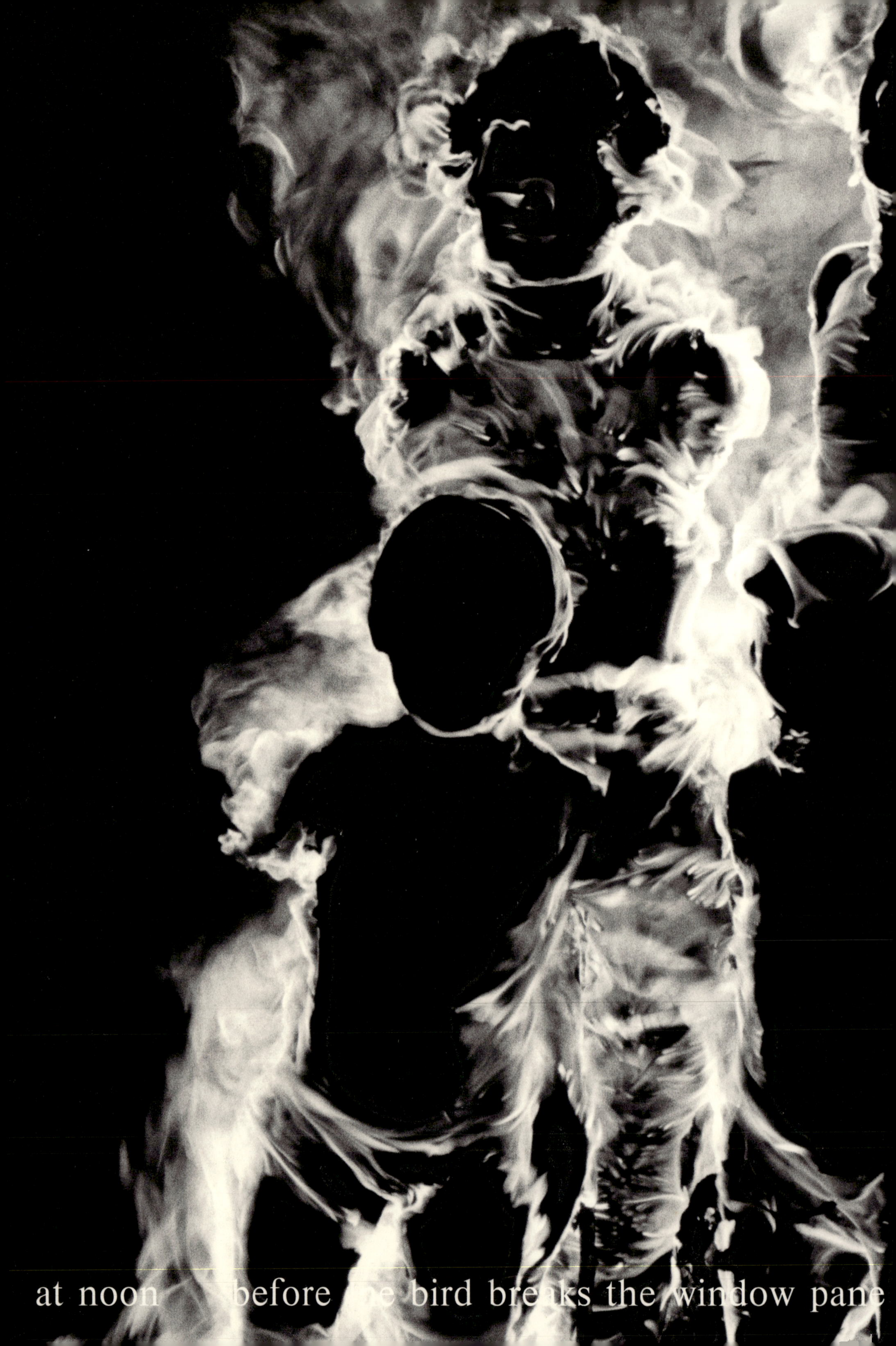

at noon   before the bird breaks the window pane

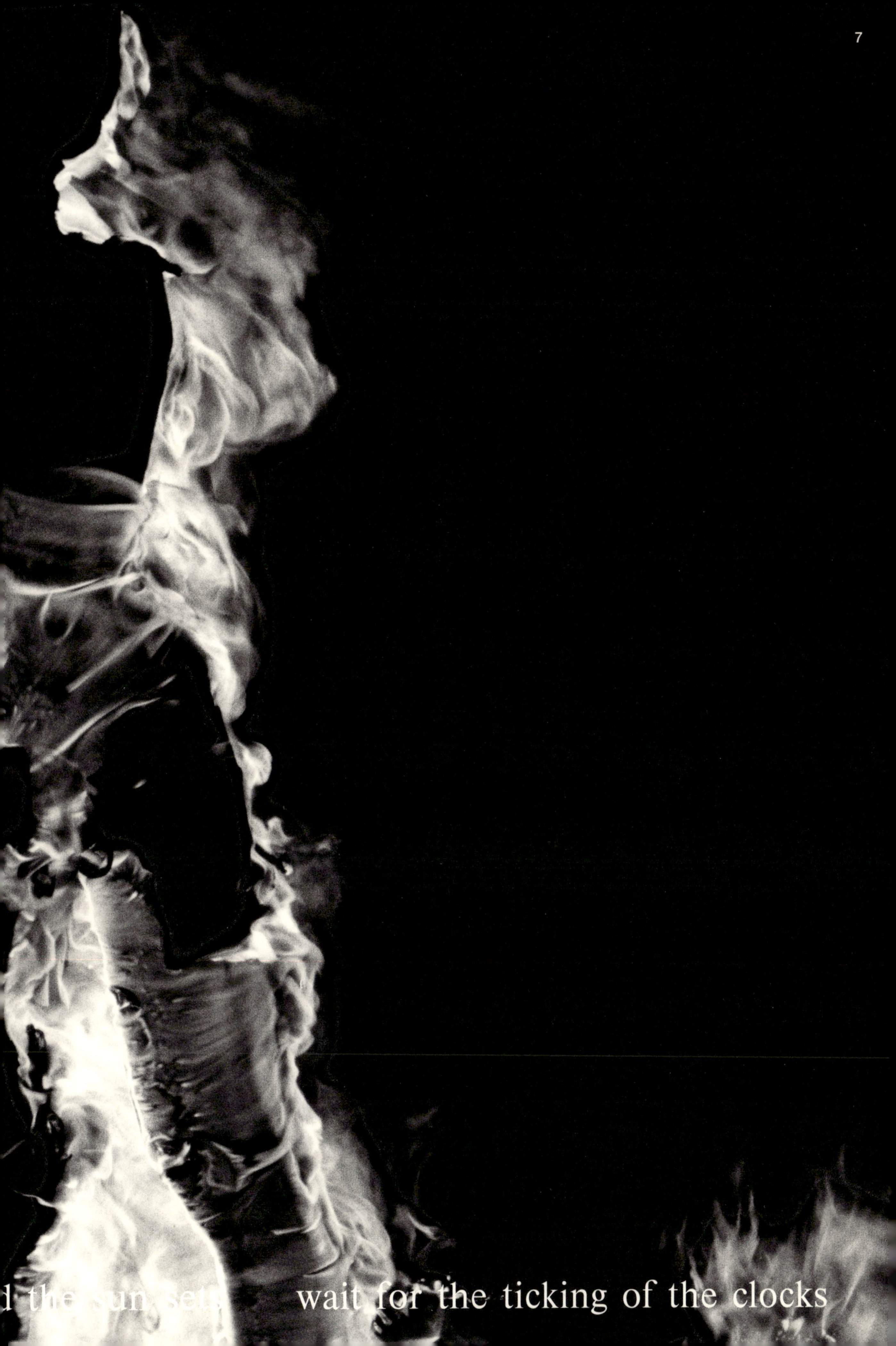

d the sun sets wait for the ticking of the clocks

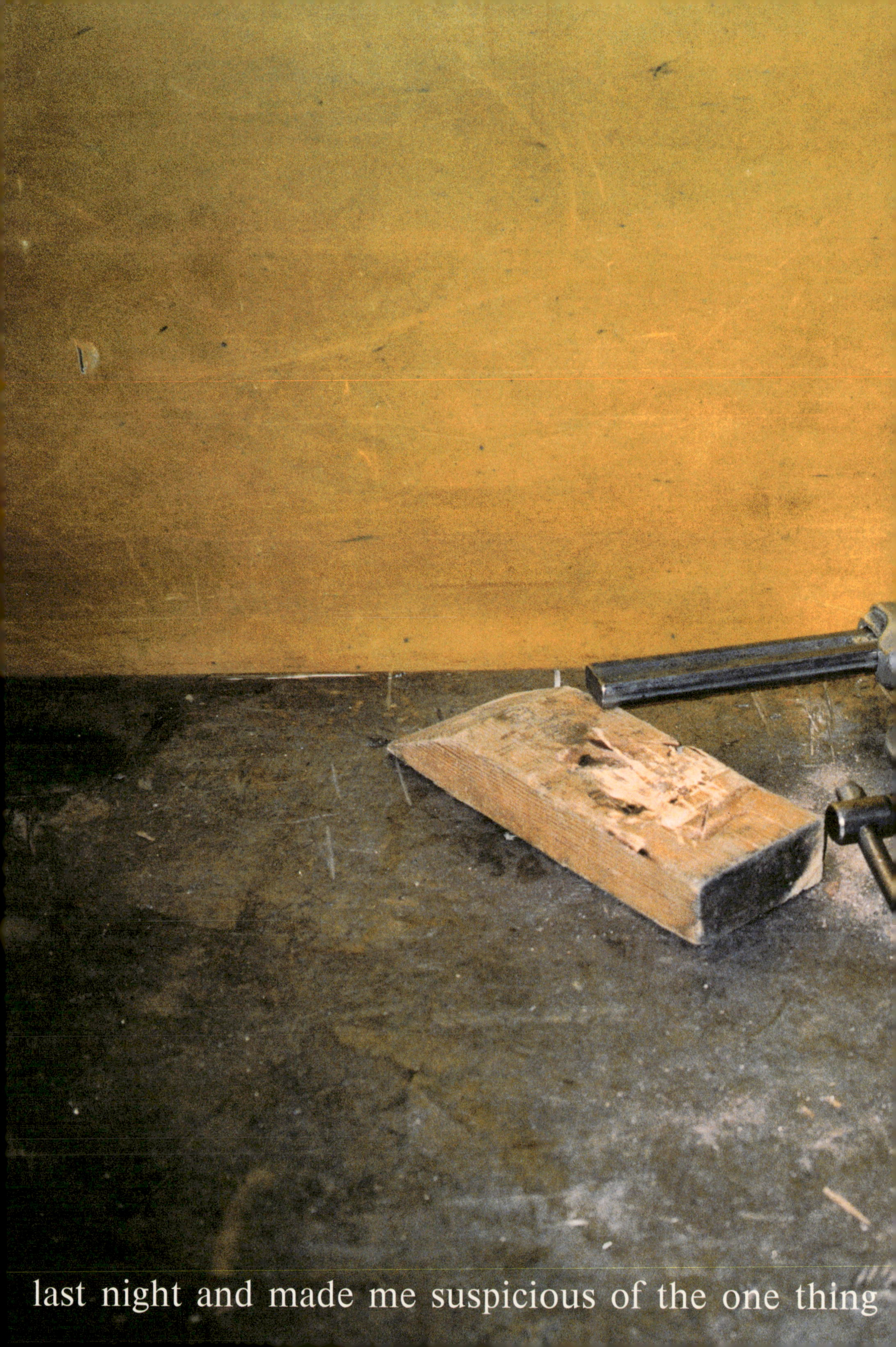

last night and made me suspicious of the one thing

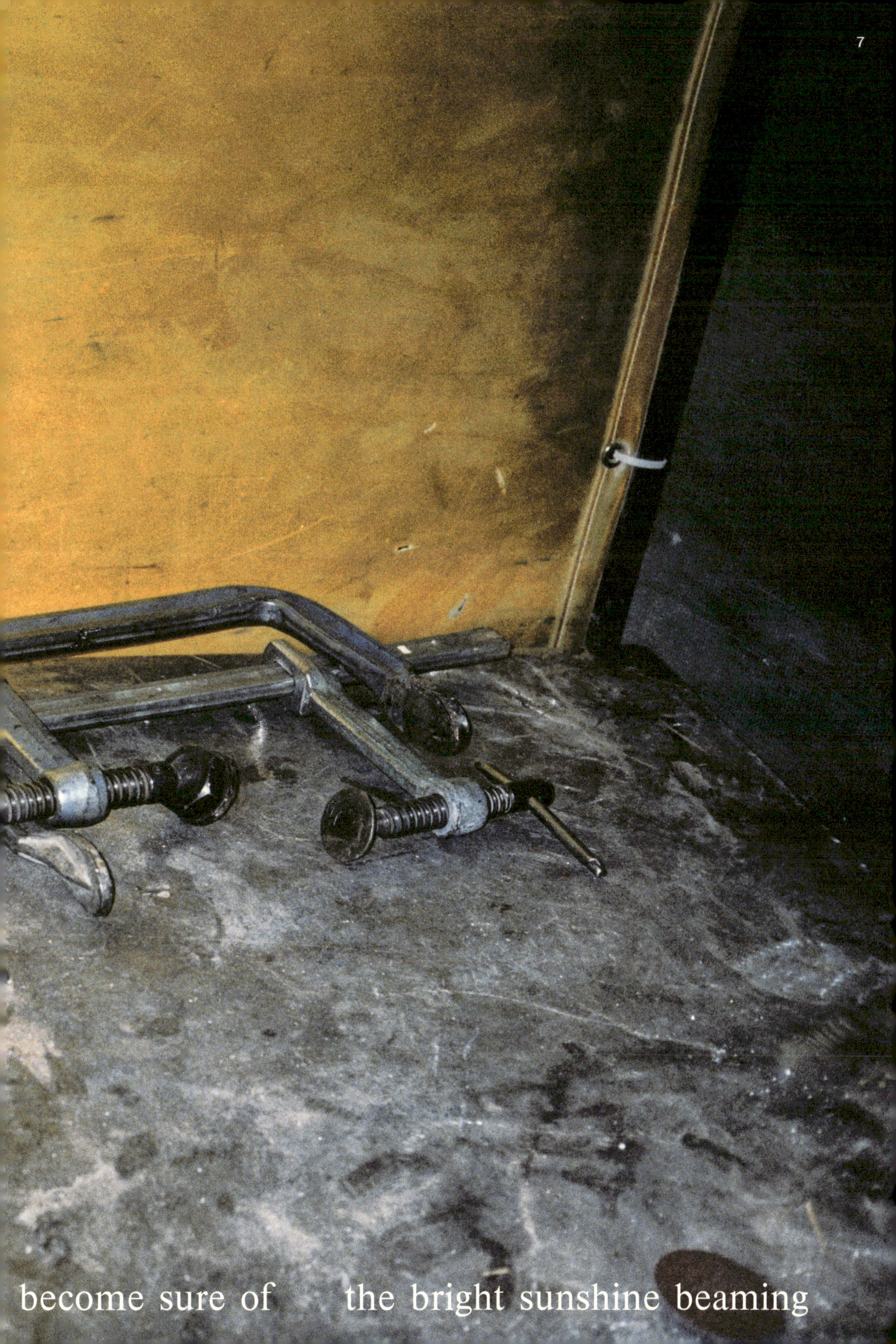

become sure of the bright sunshine beaming

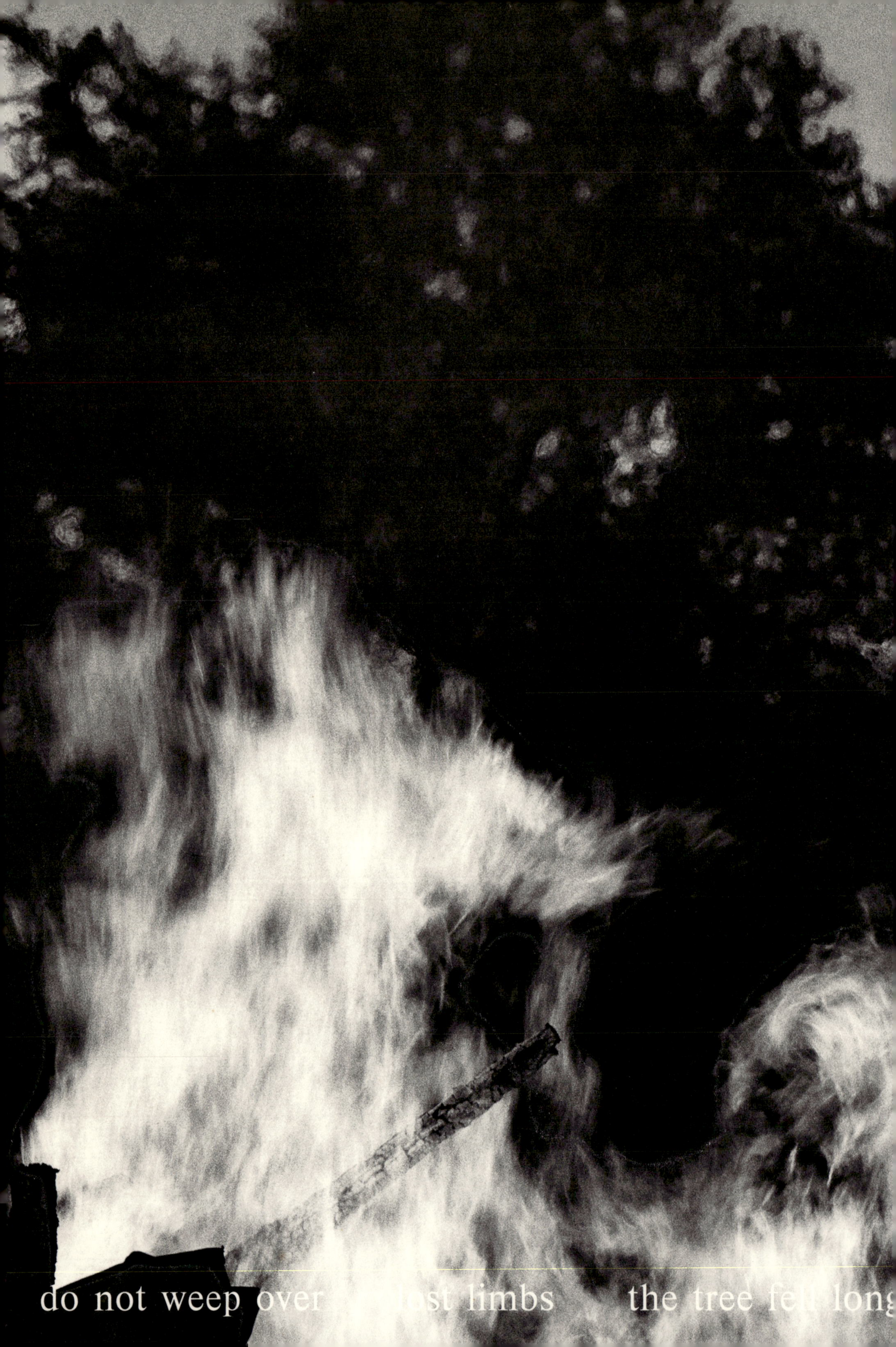
do not weep over lost limbs the tree felt long

o alone in the fireworks eyes only for the

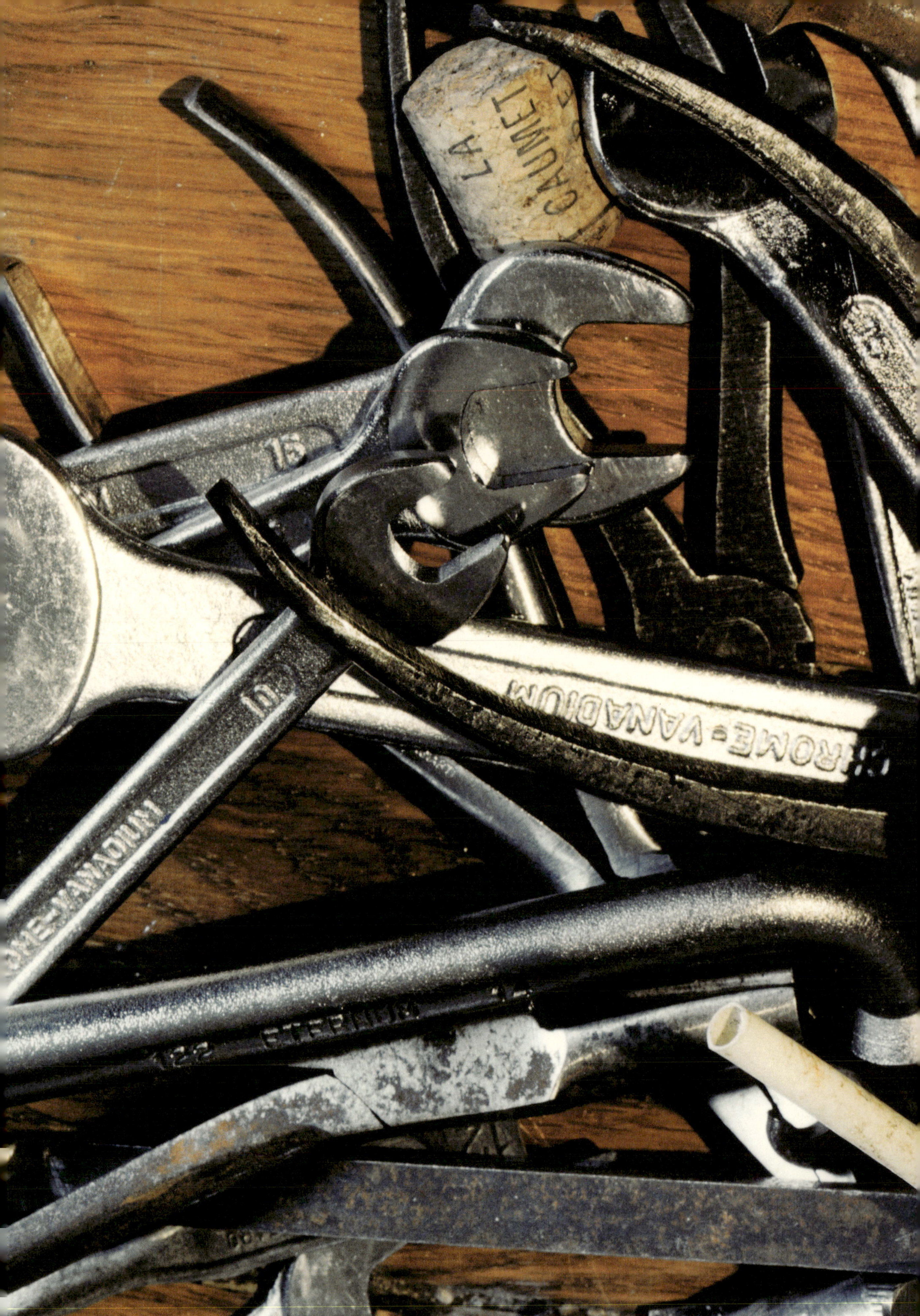

focused on new york   direct from you and w

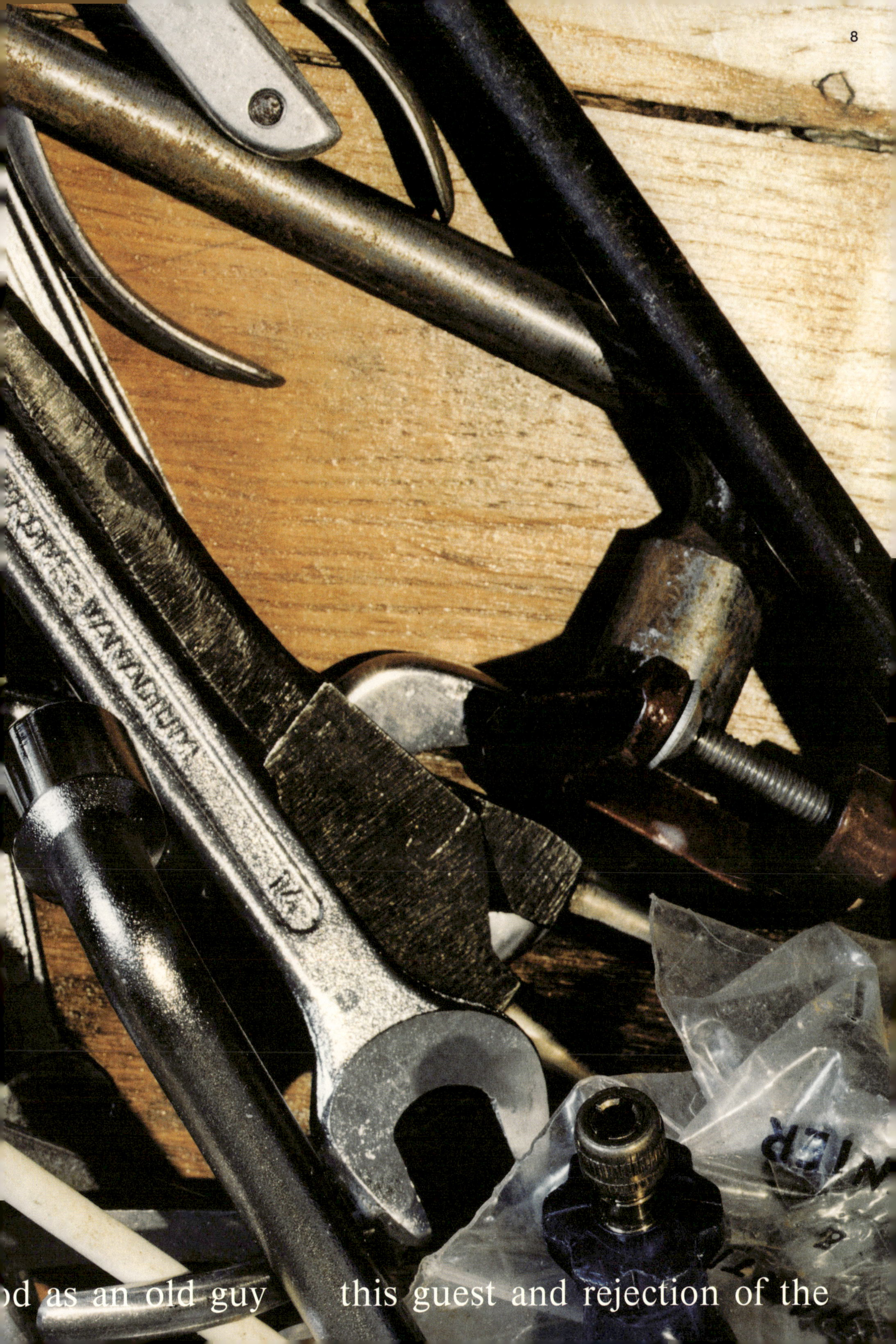

od as an old guy this guest and rejection of the

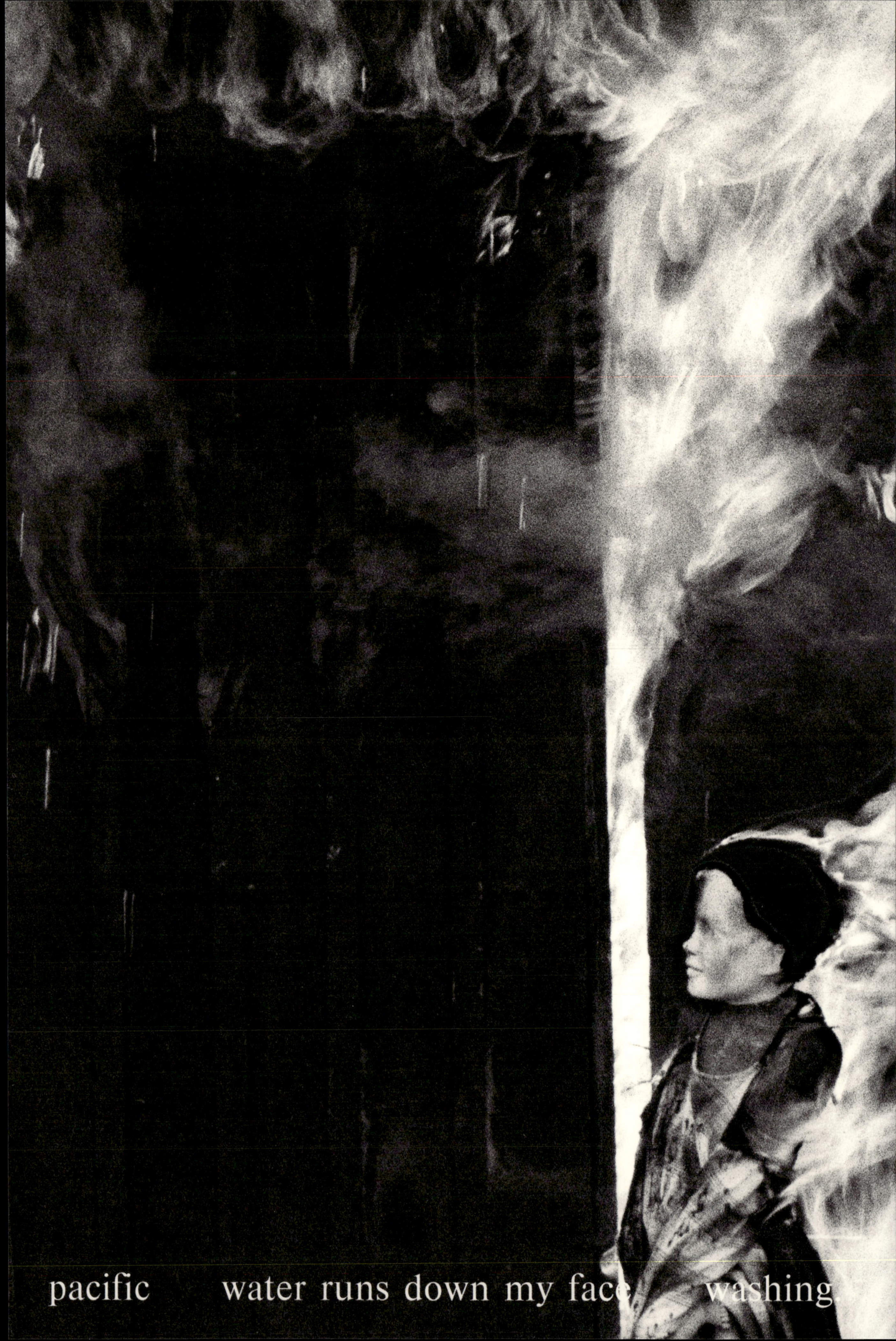

pacific water runs down my face washing.

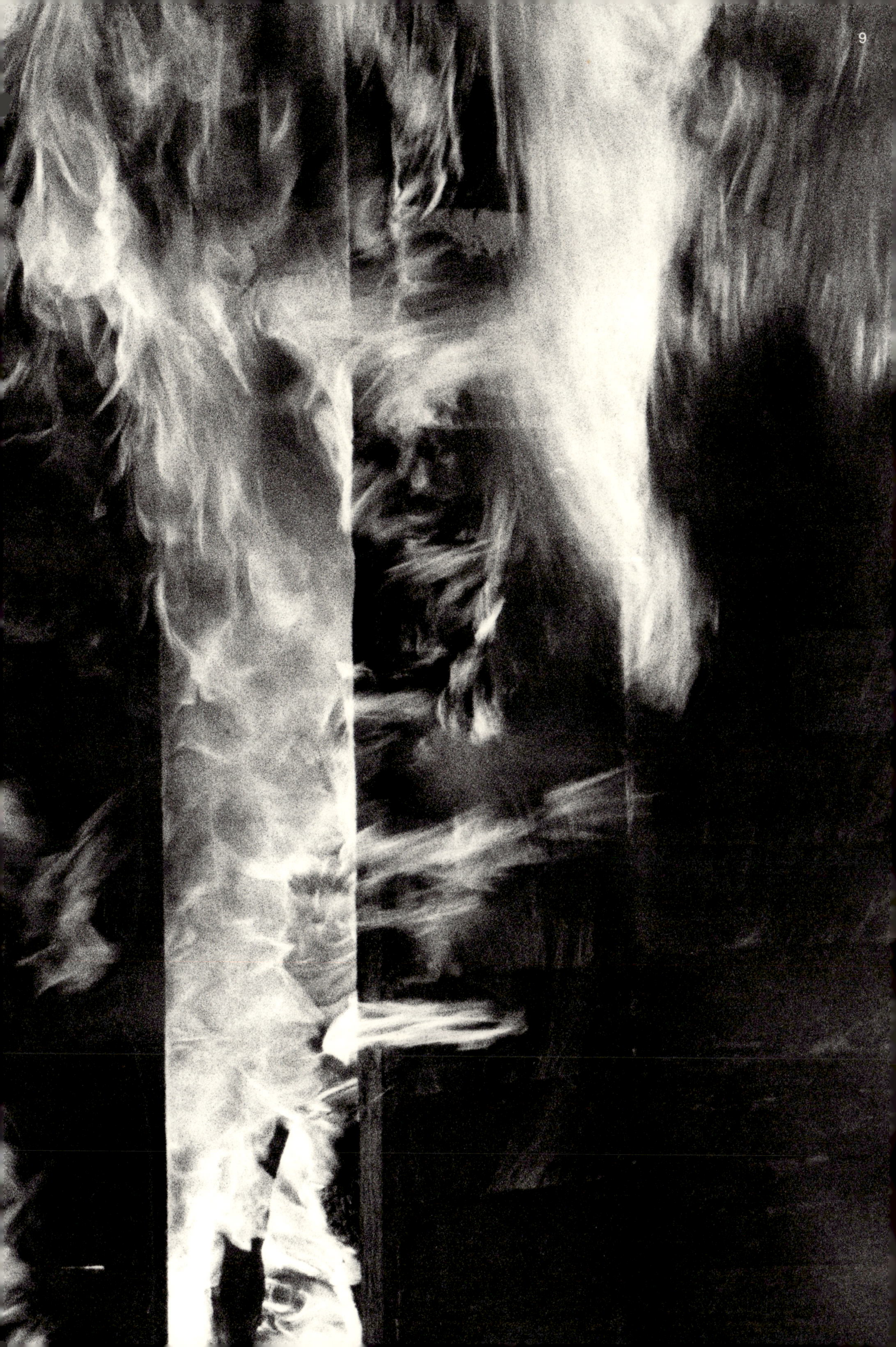

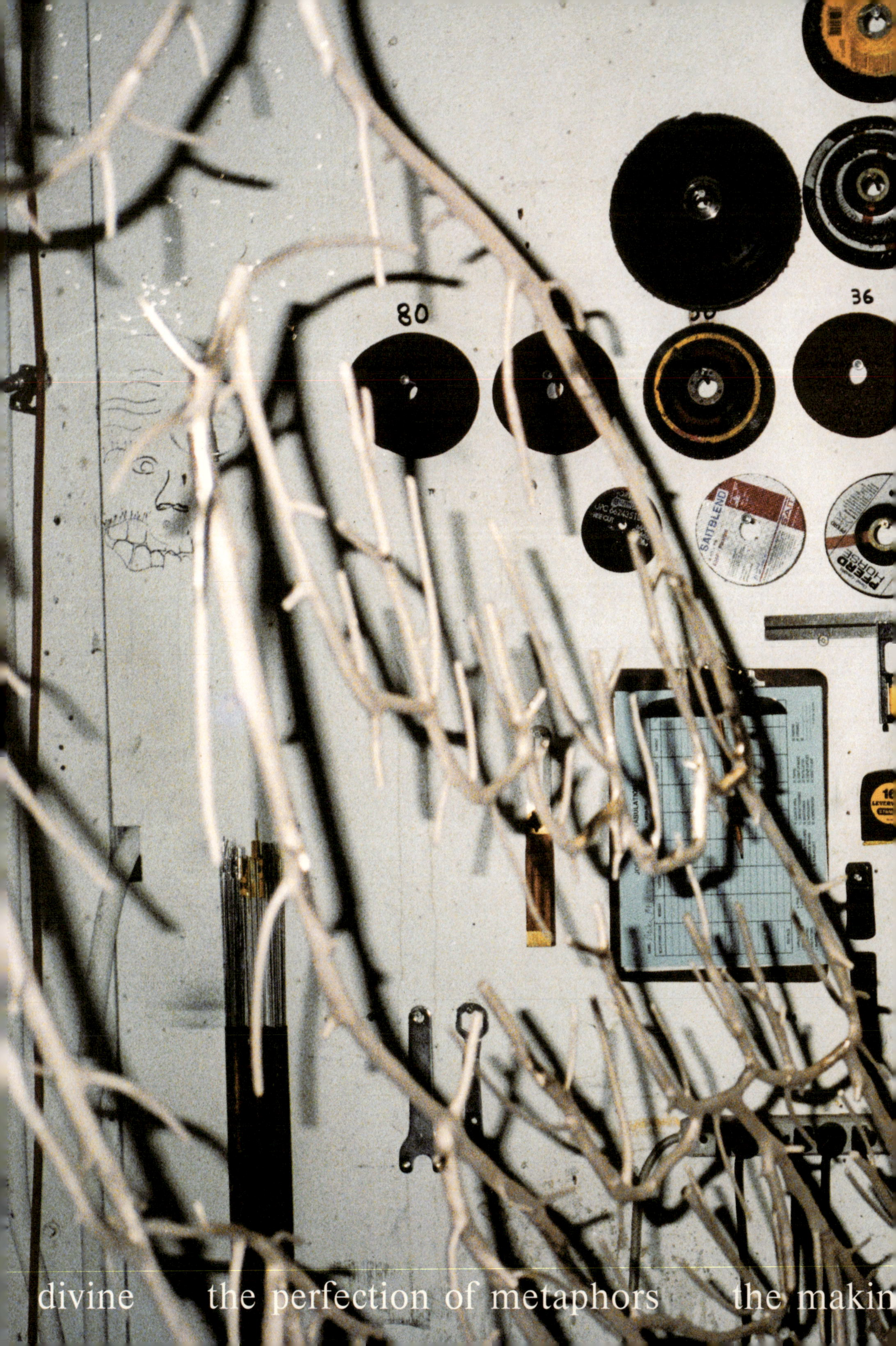

divine the perfection of metaphors the makin

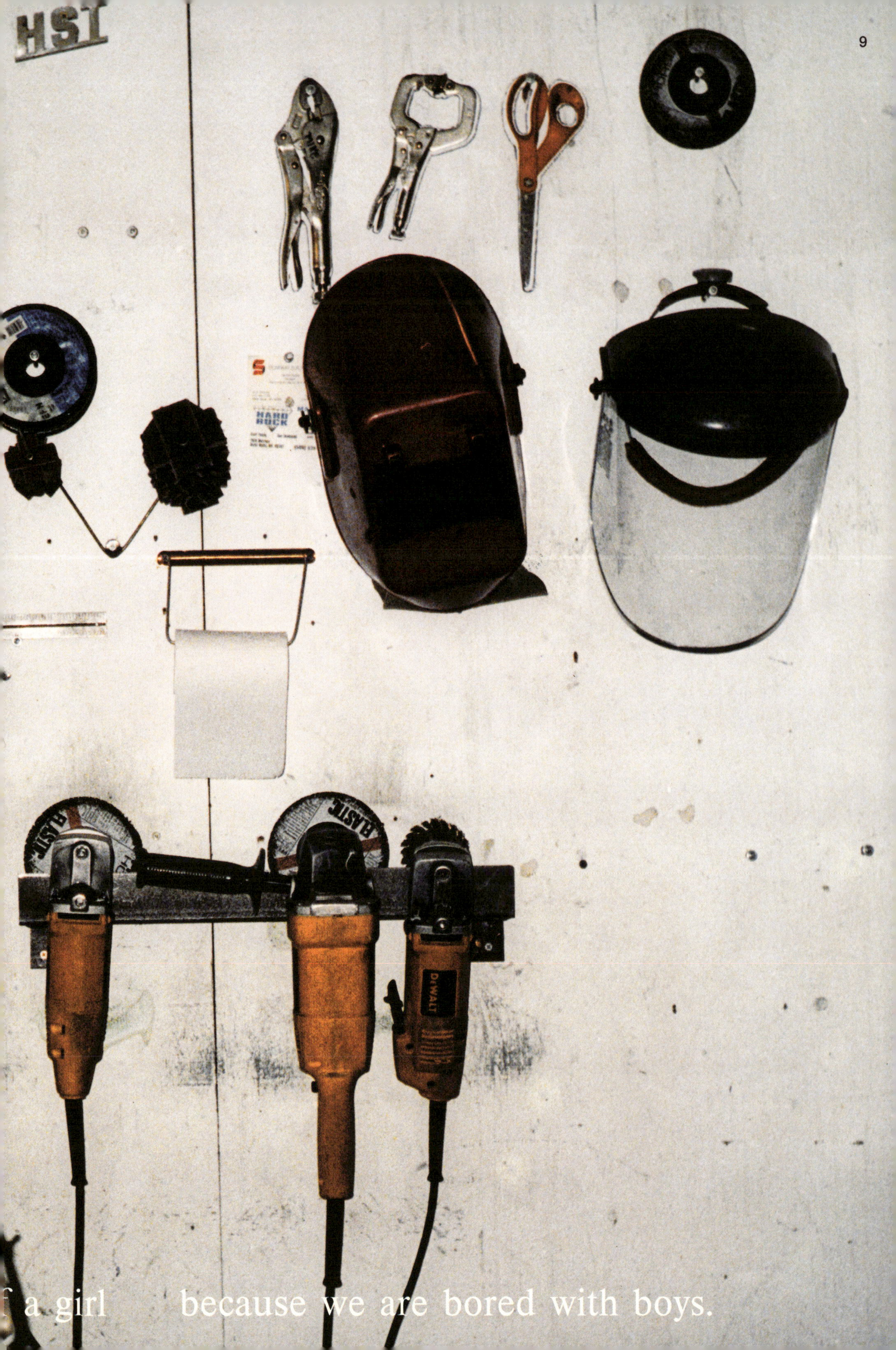

f a girl because we are bored with boys.

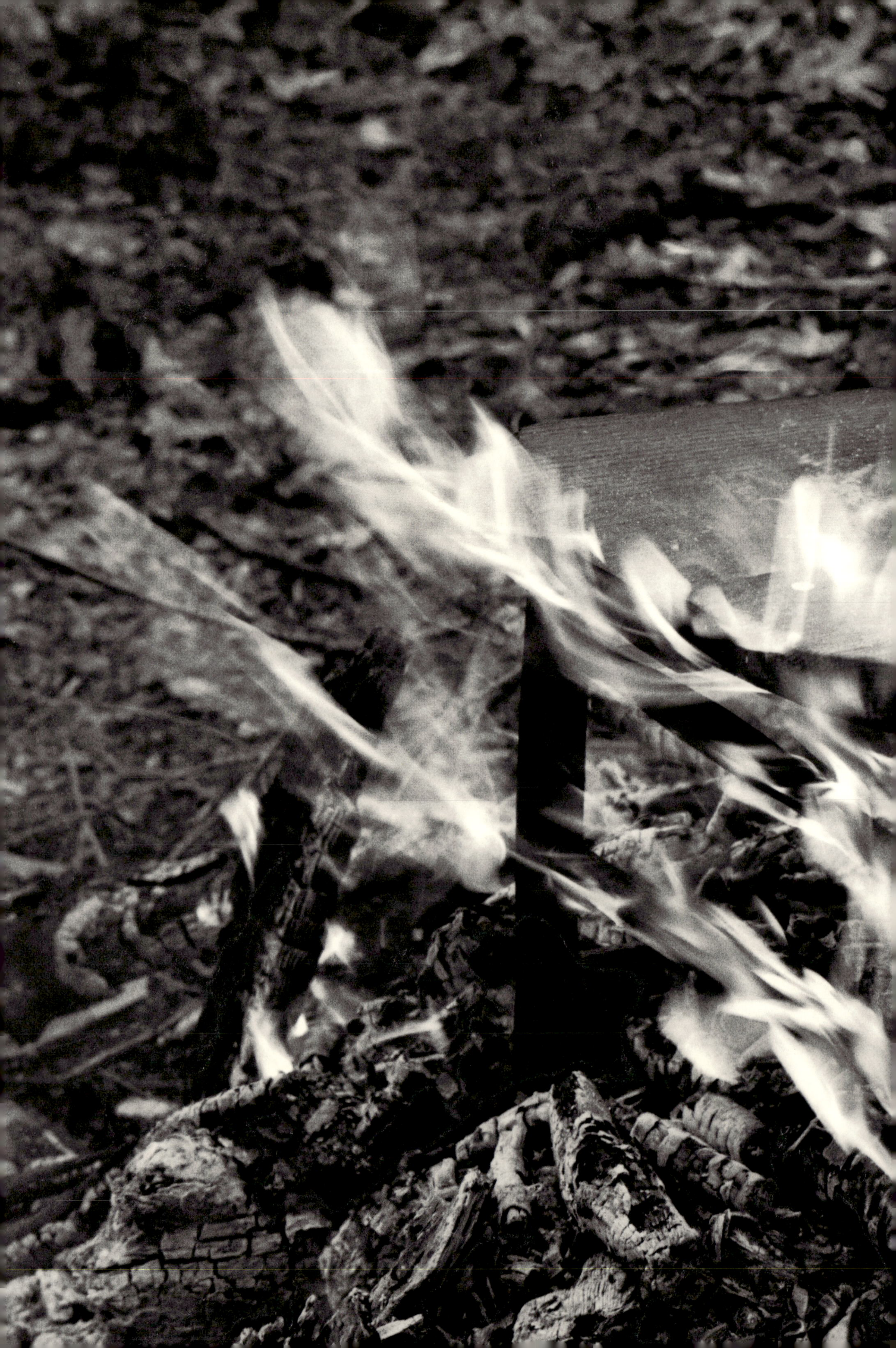

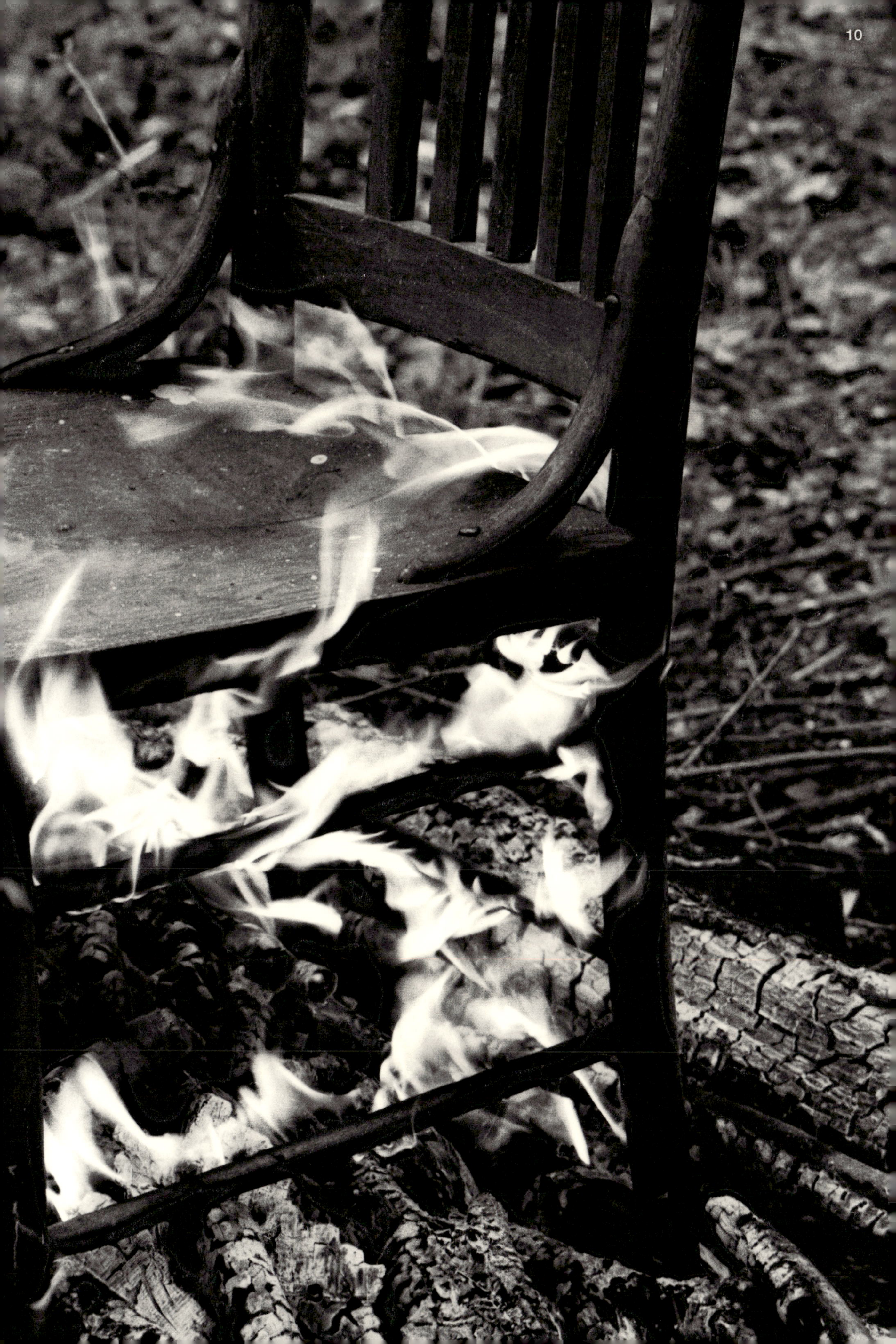

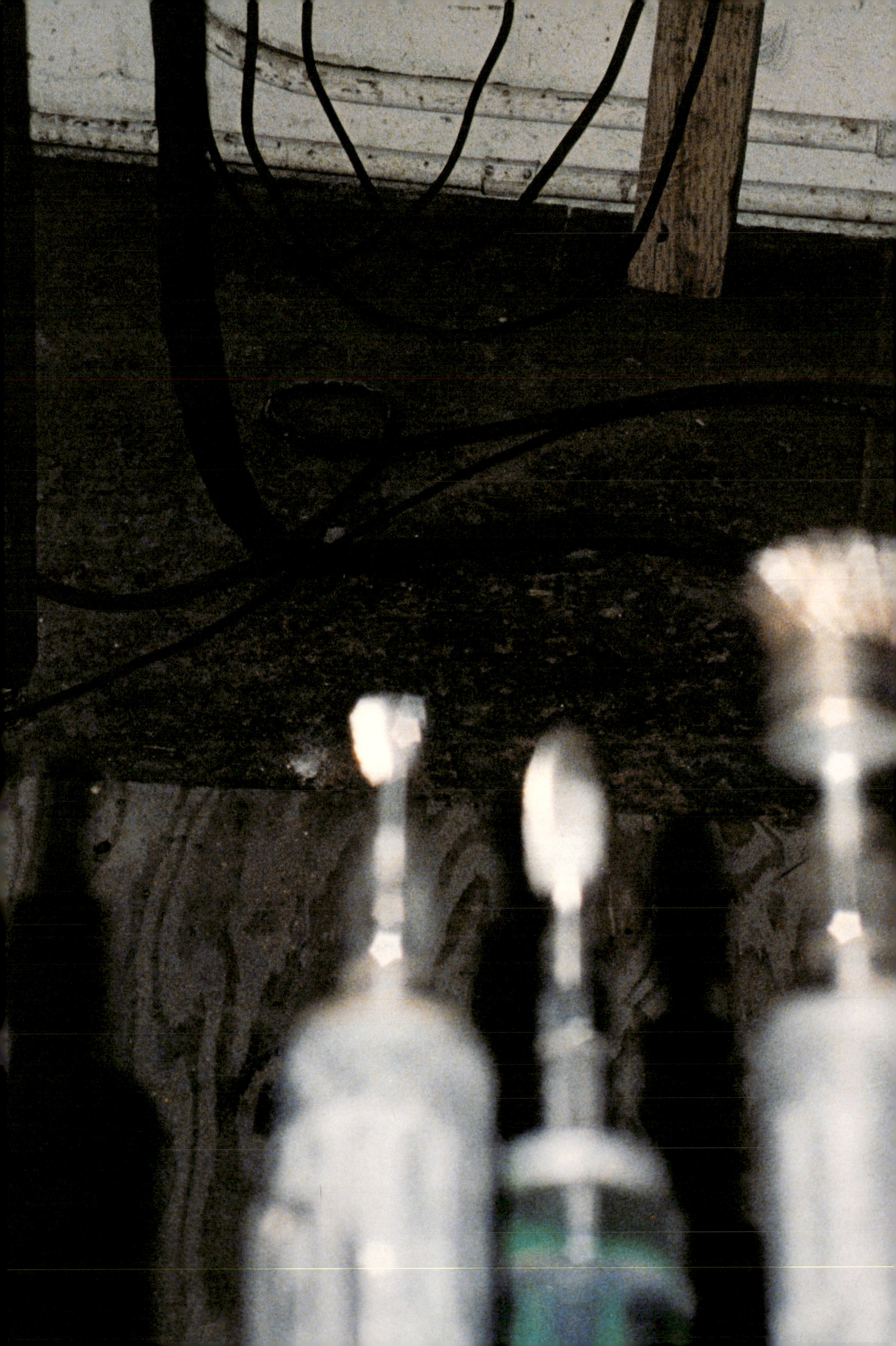

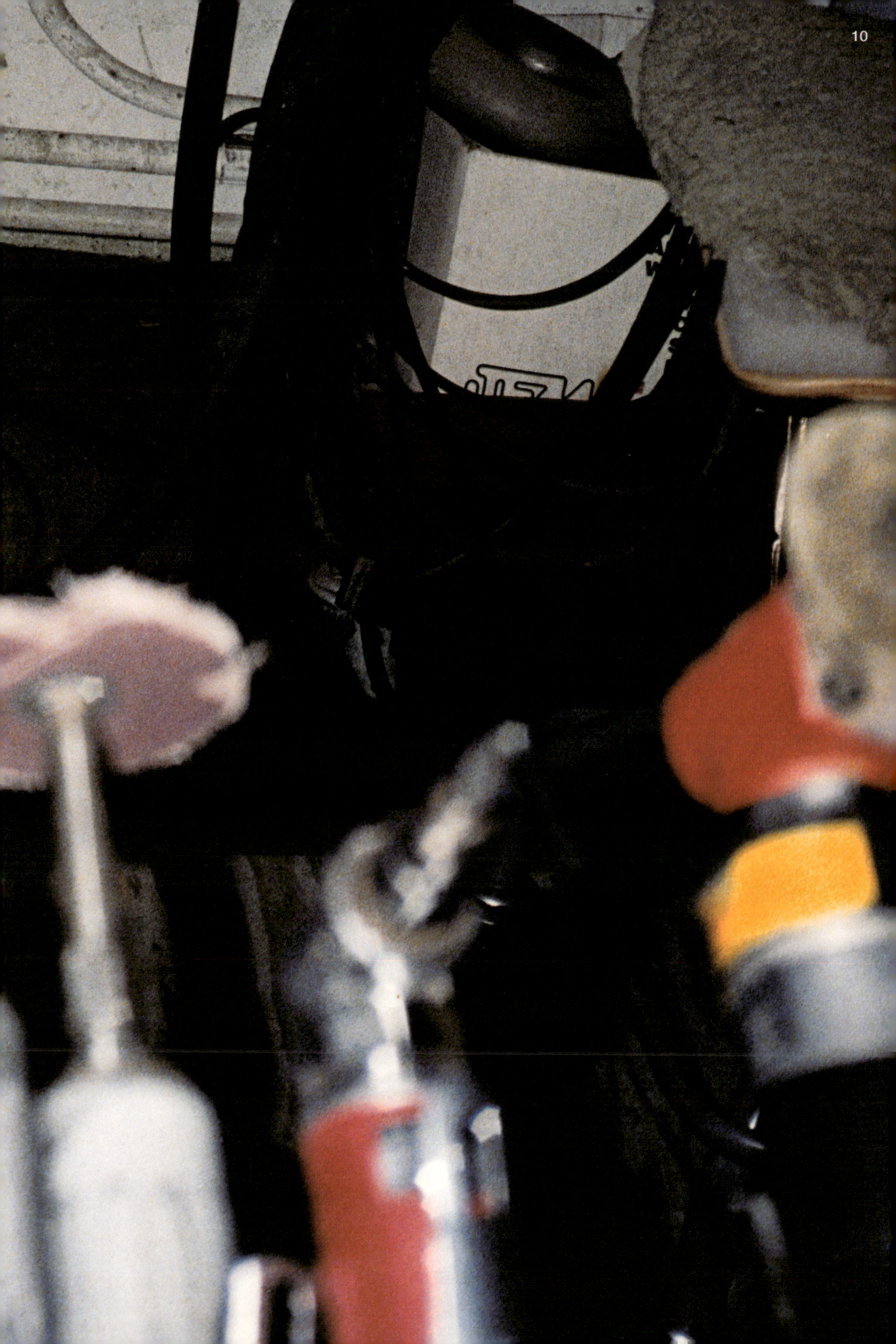

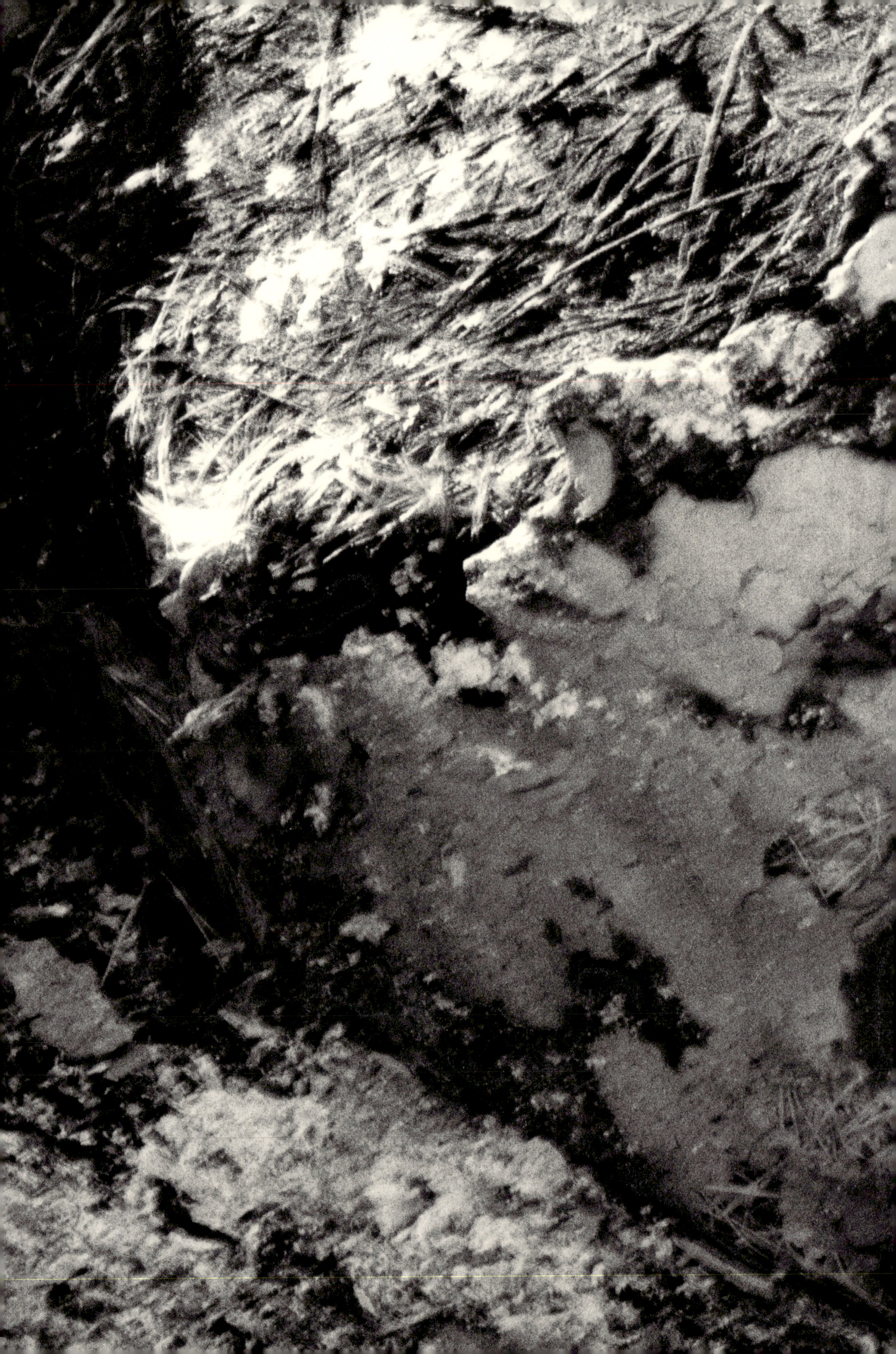

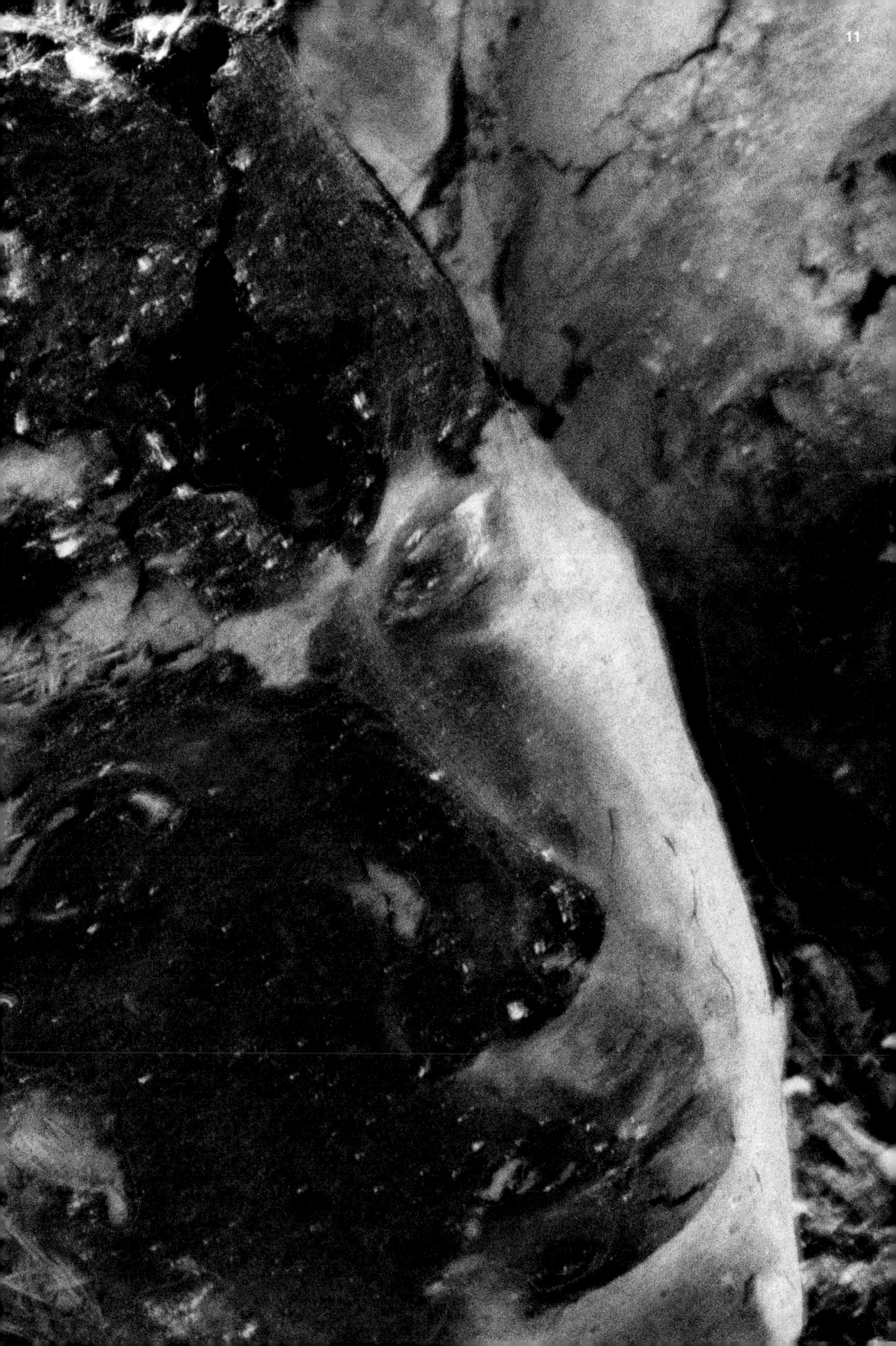

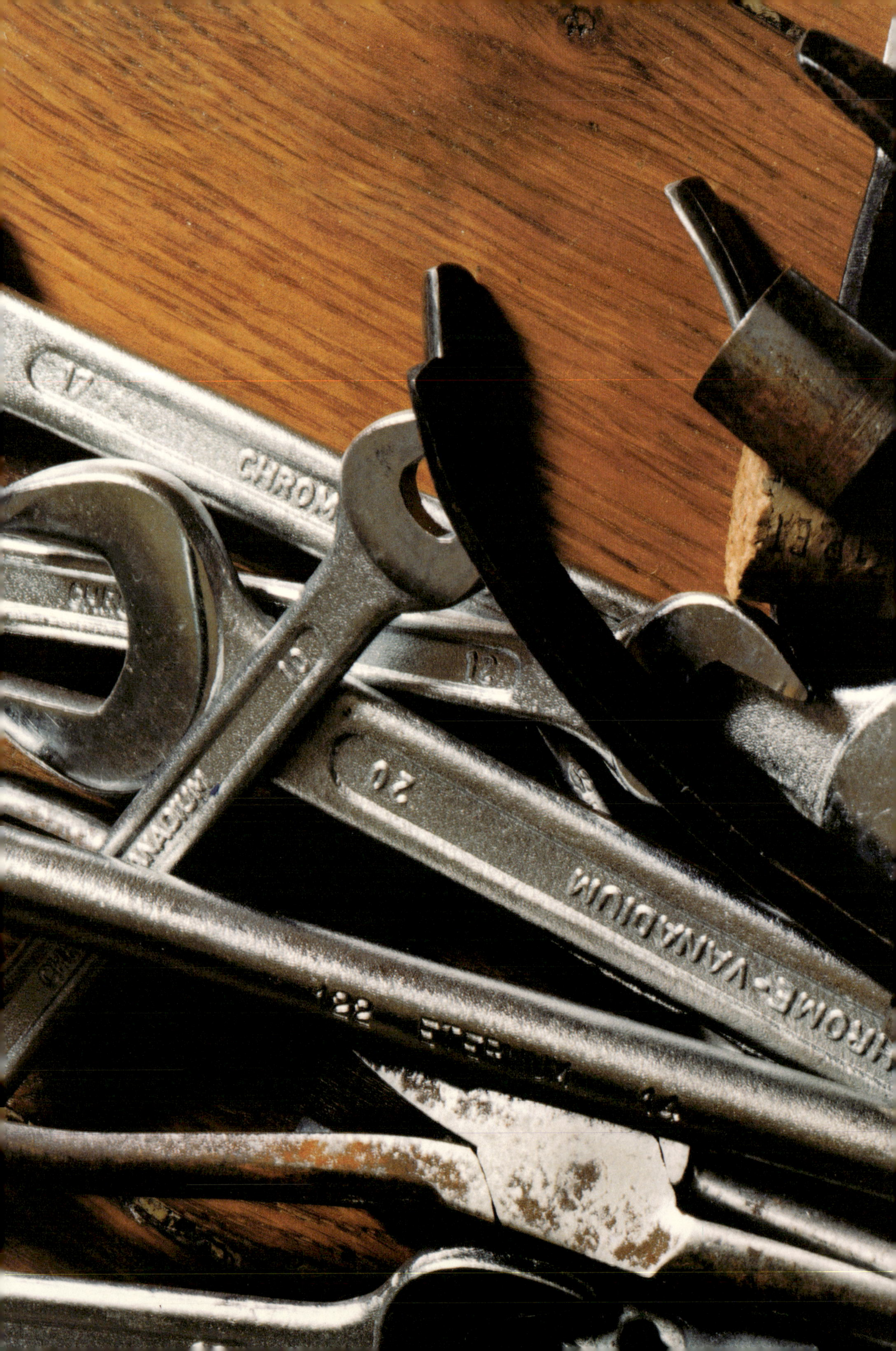

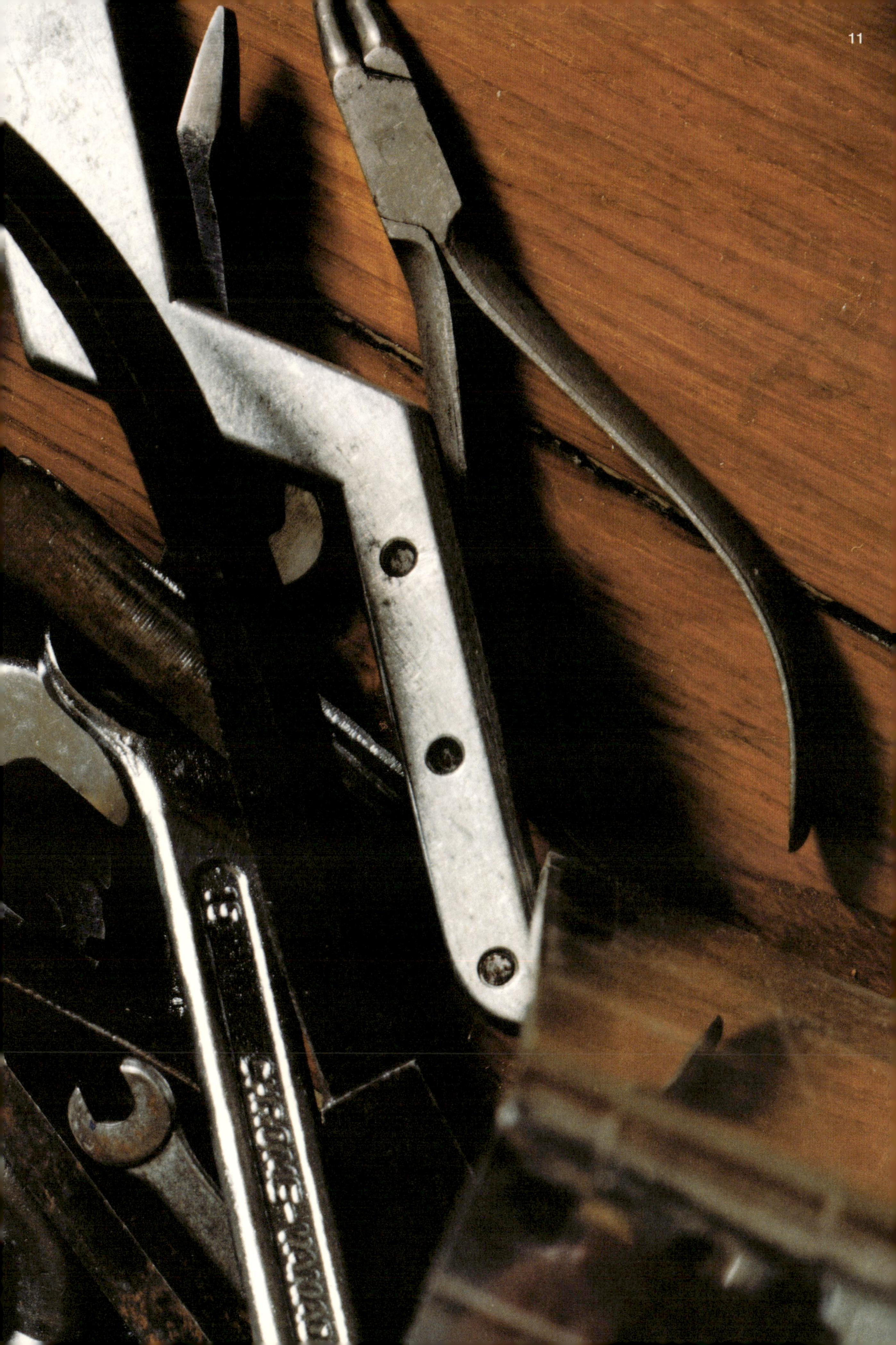

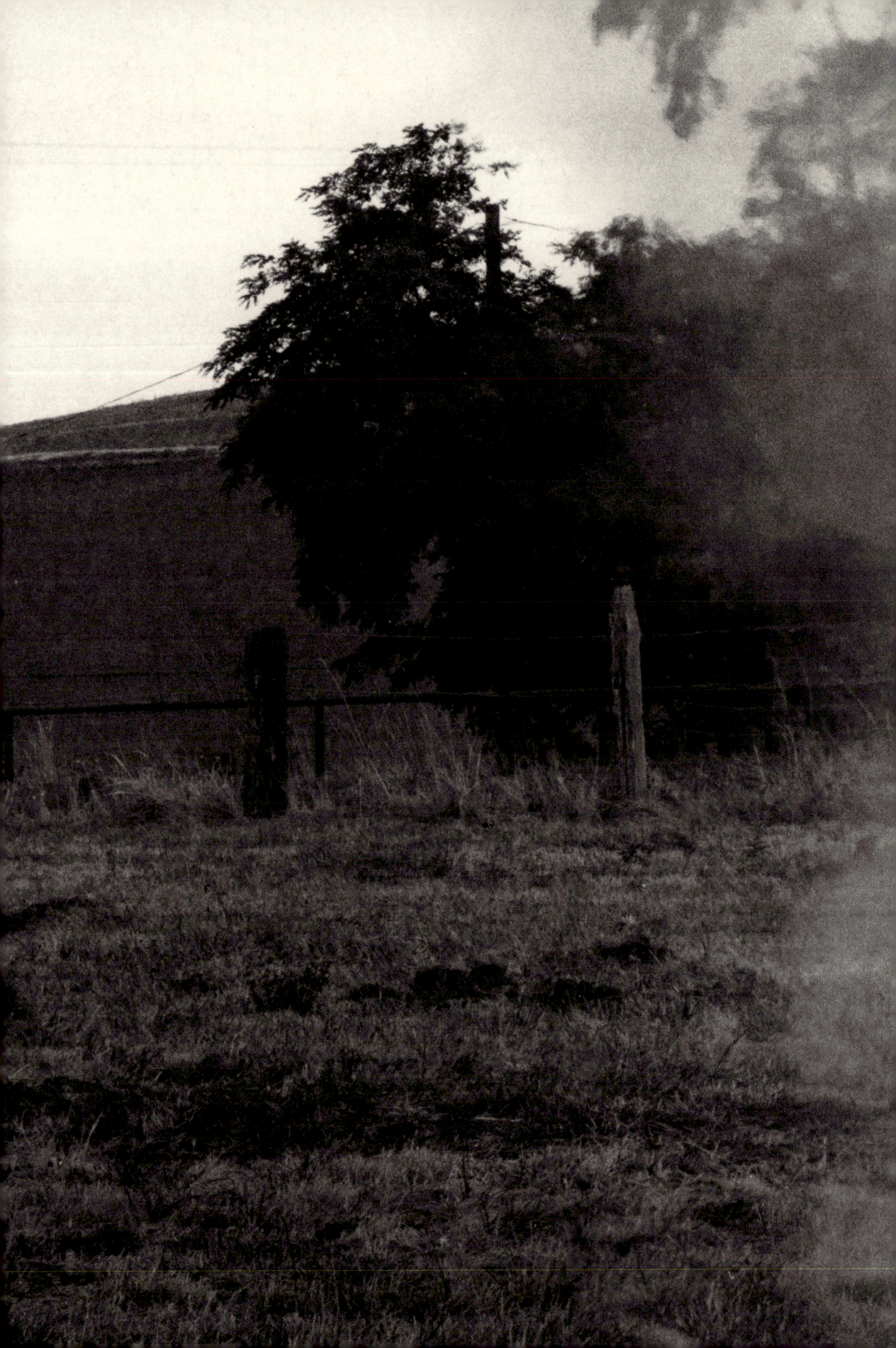

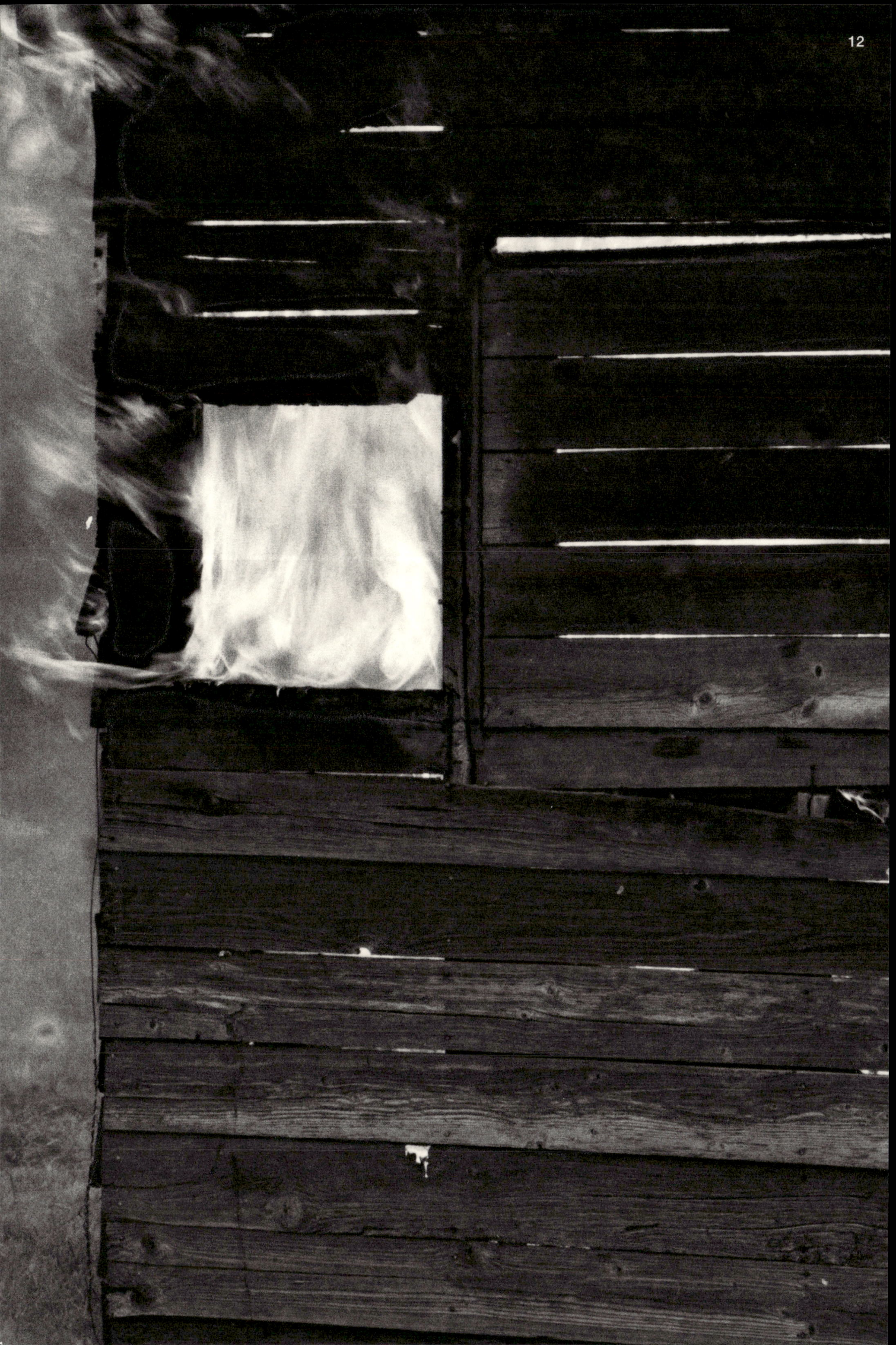

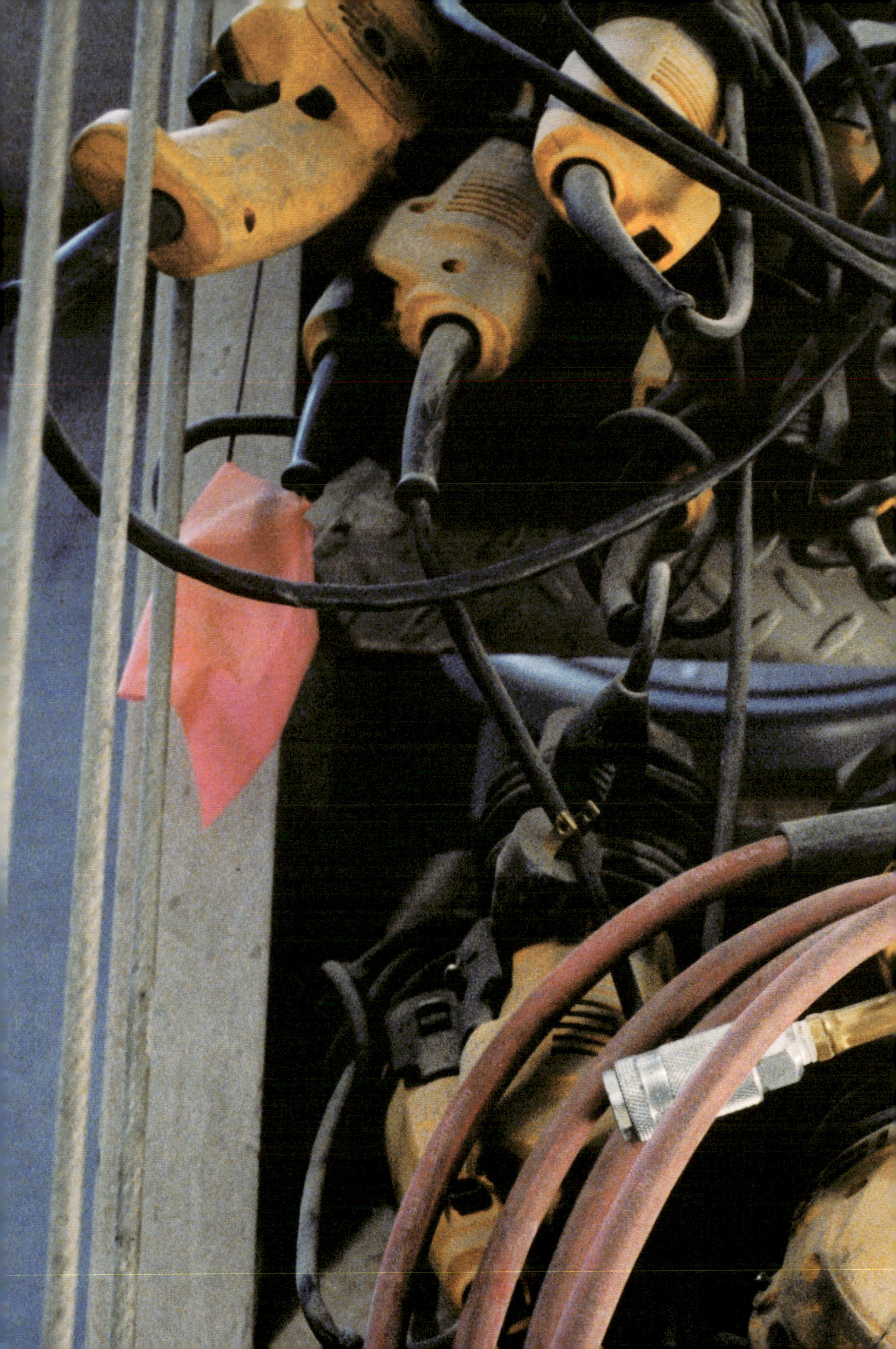

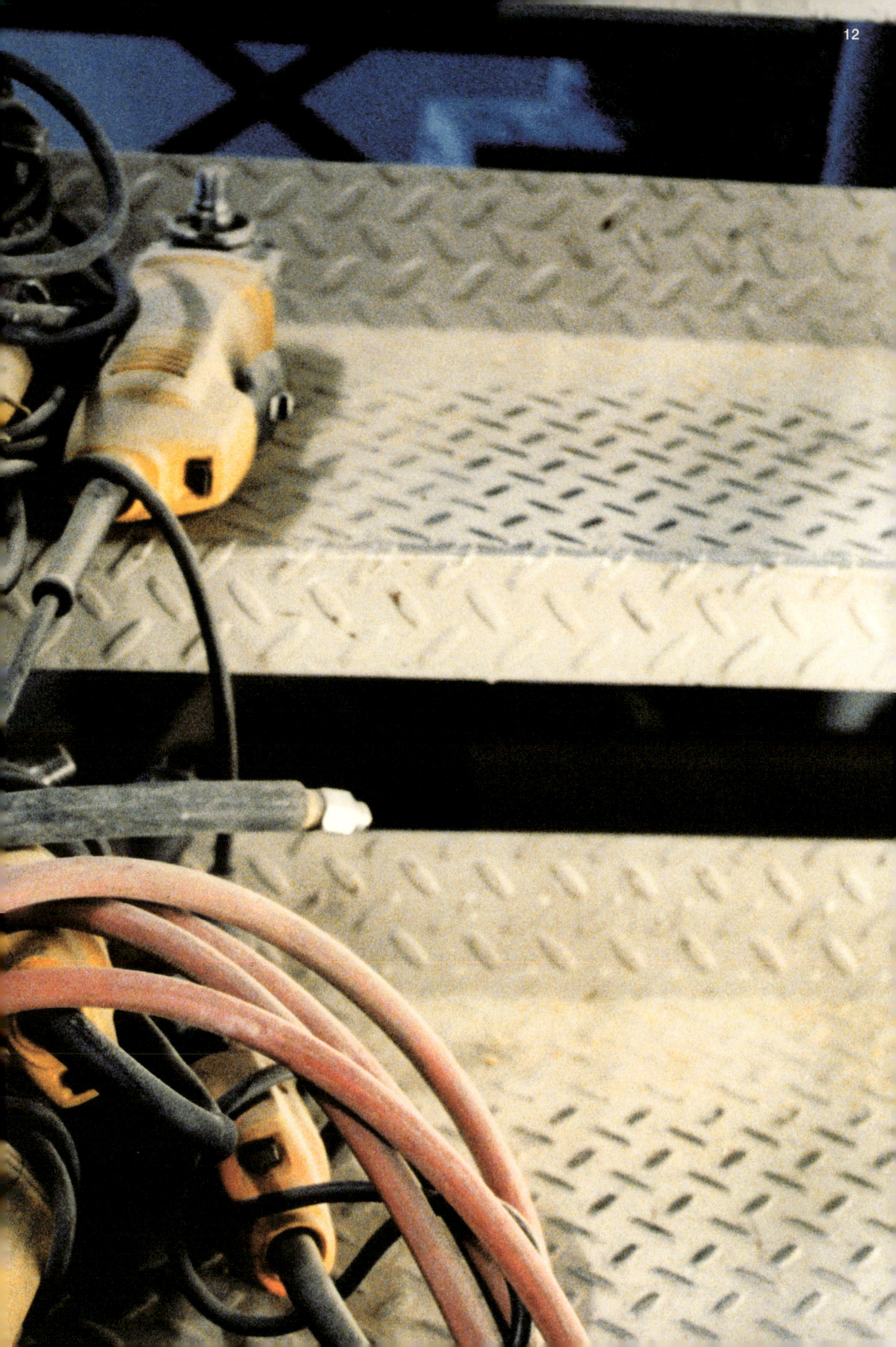

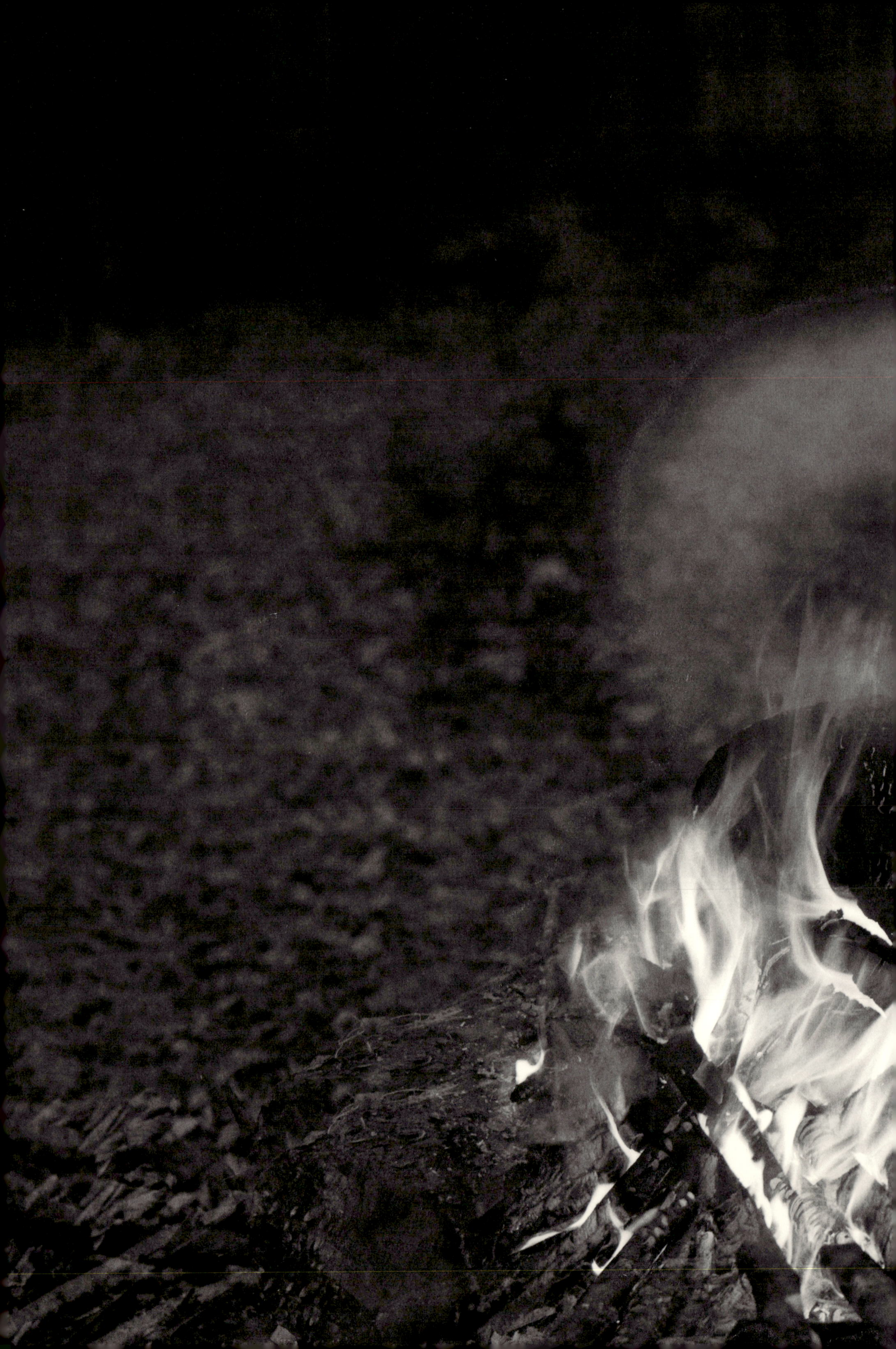

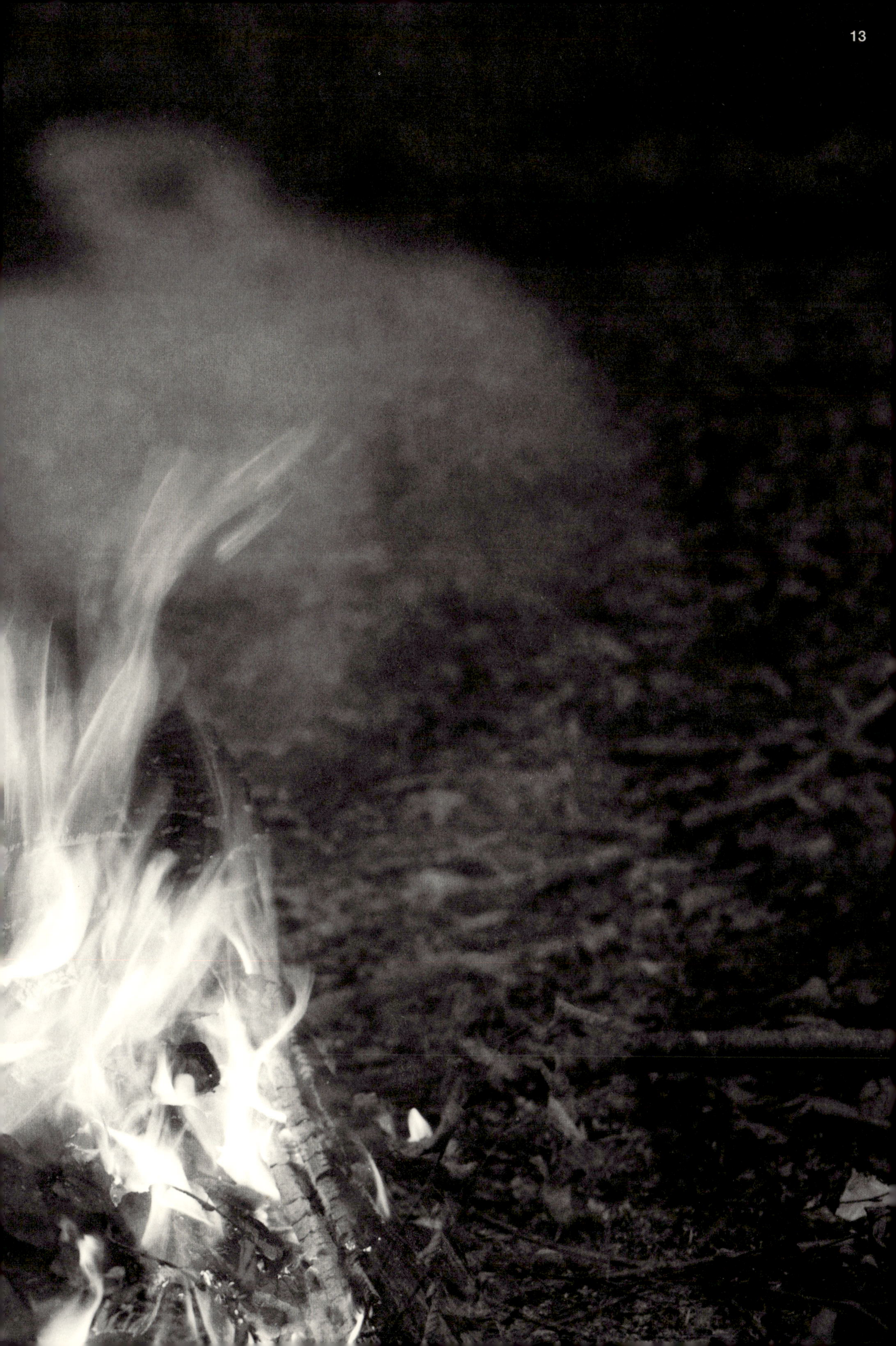

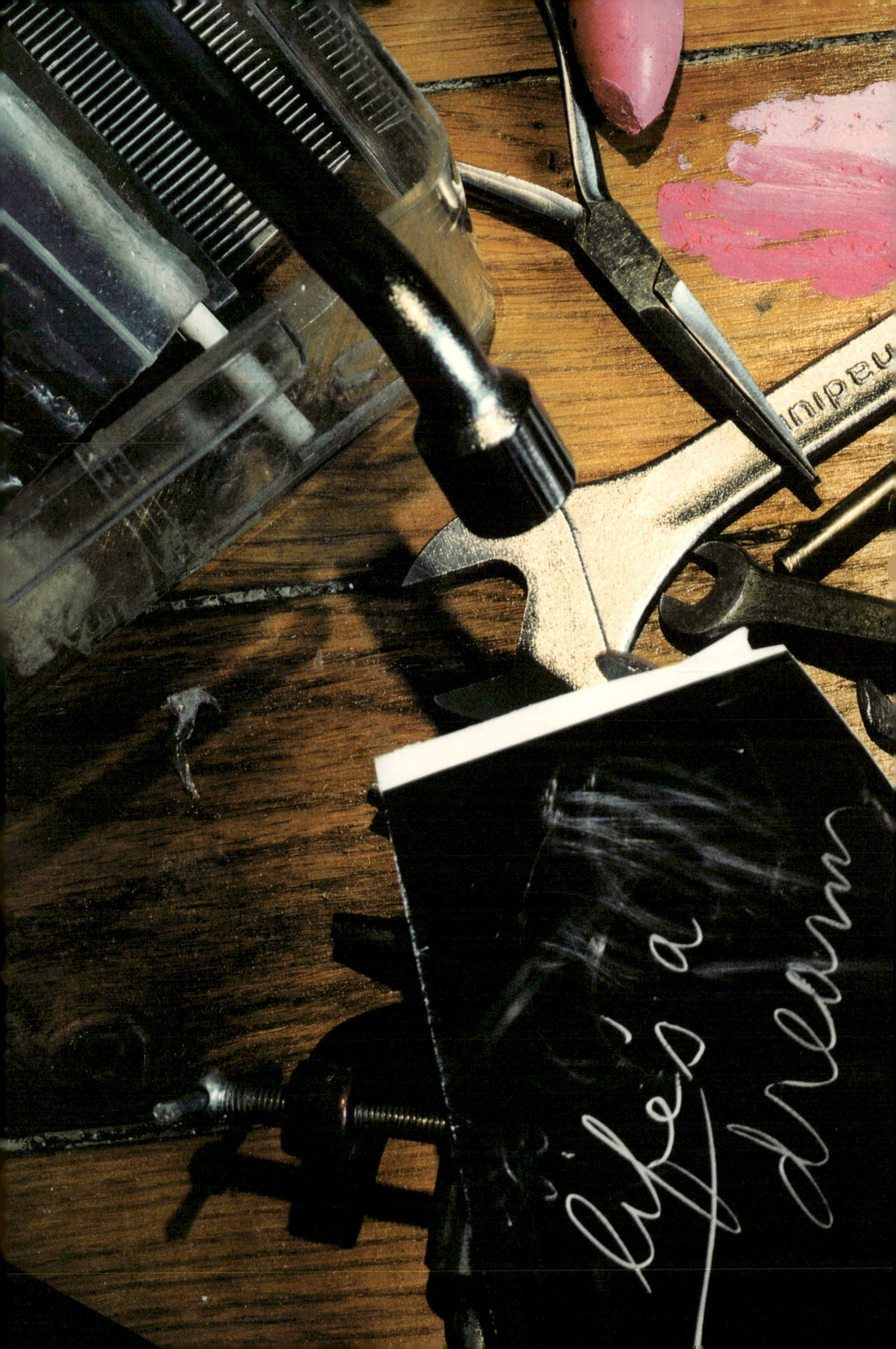
life's a dream

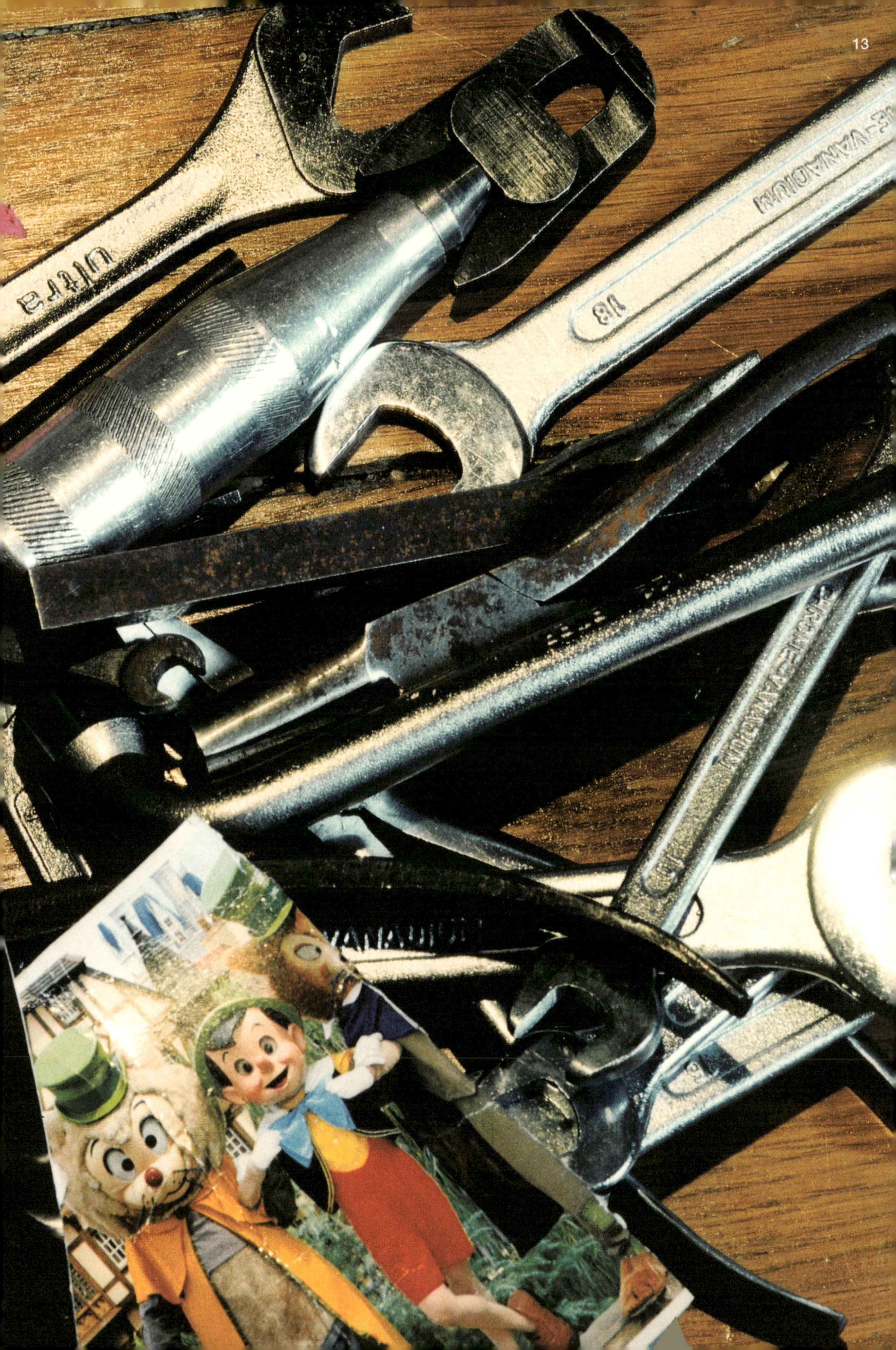

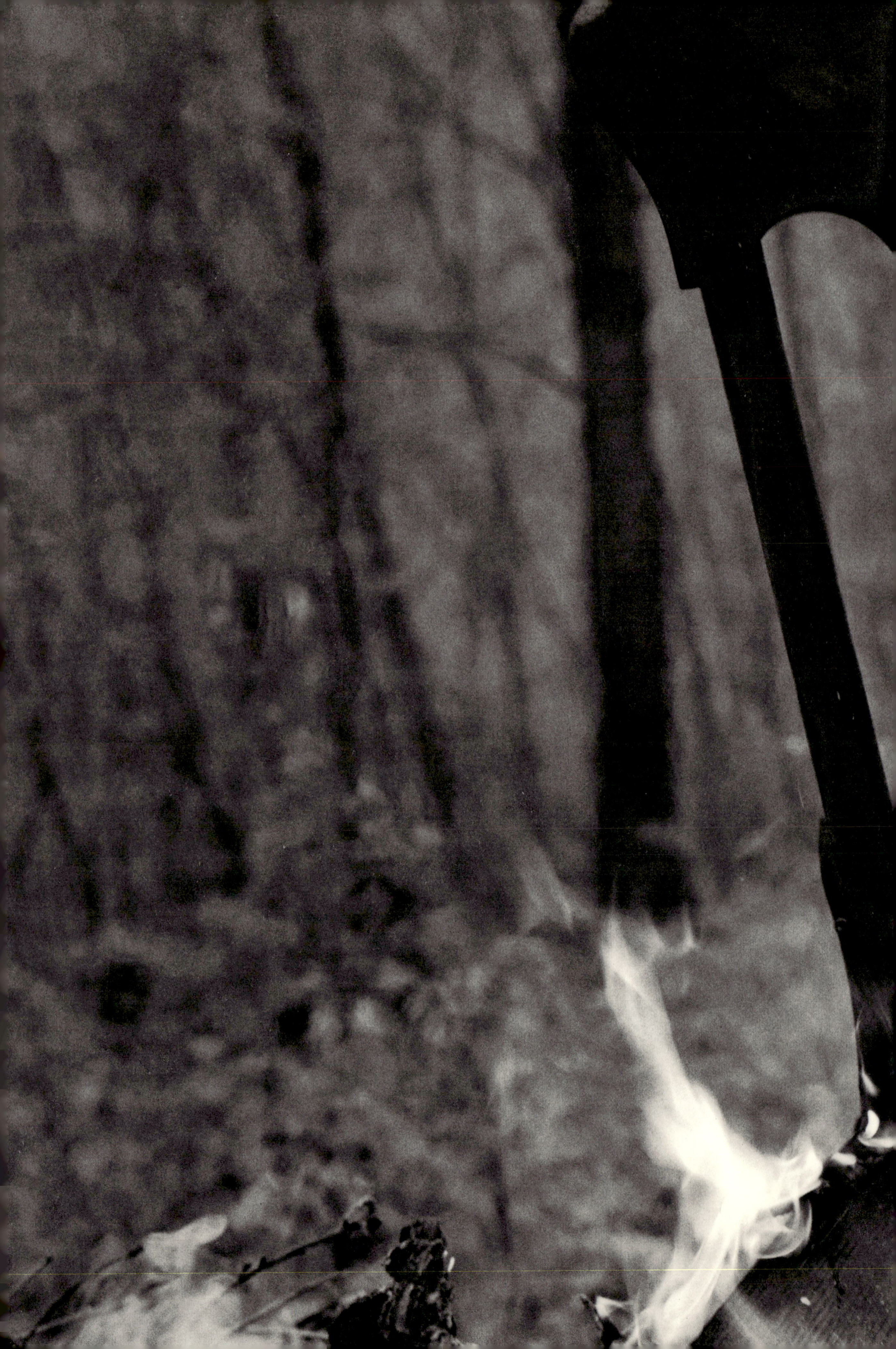

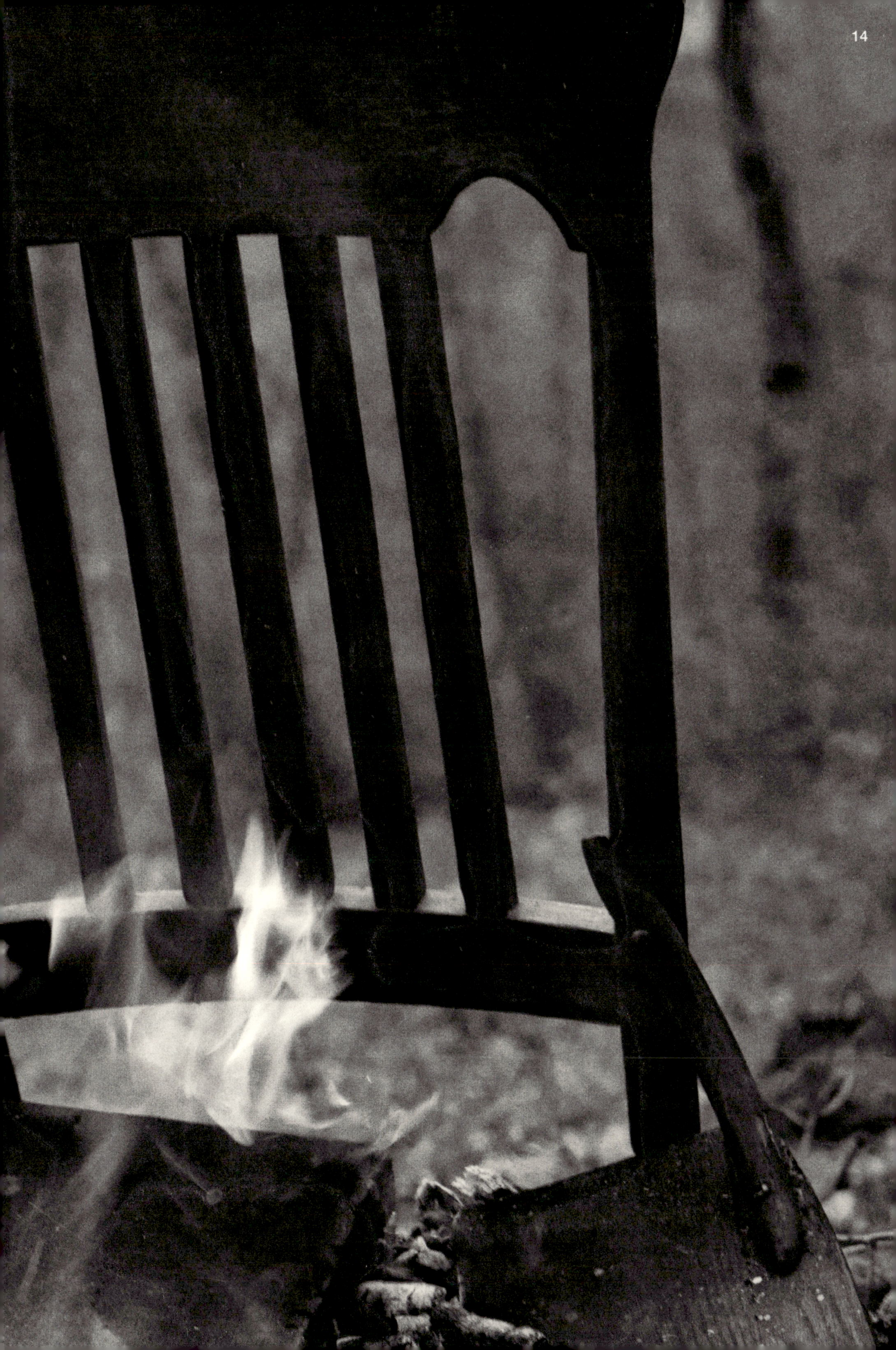

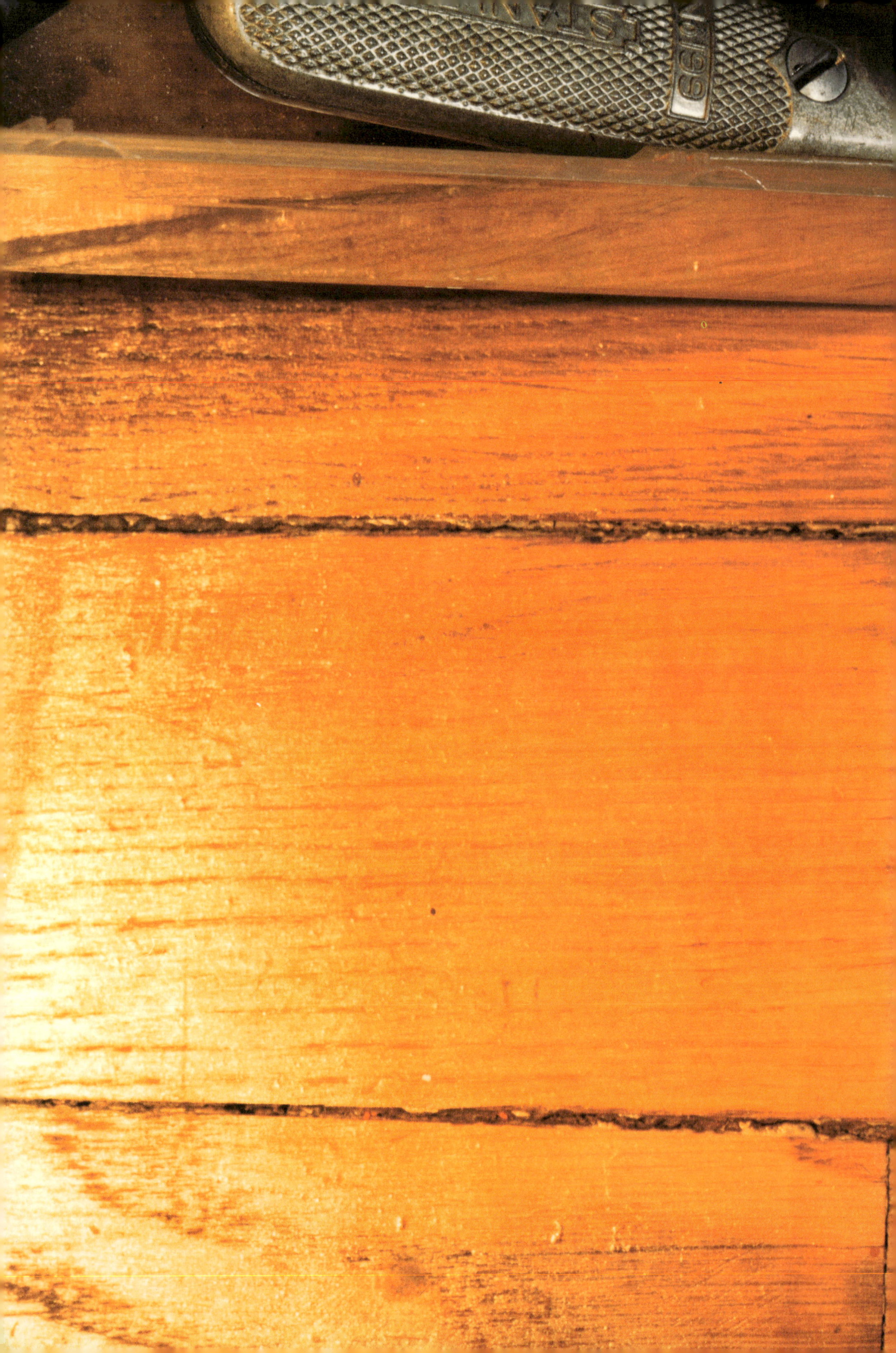

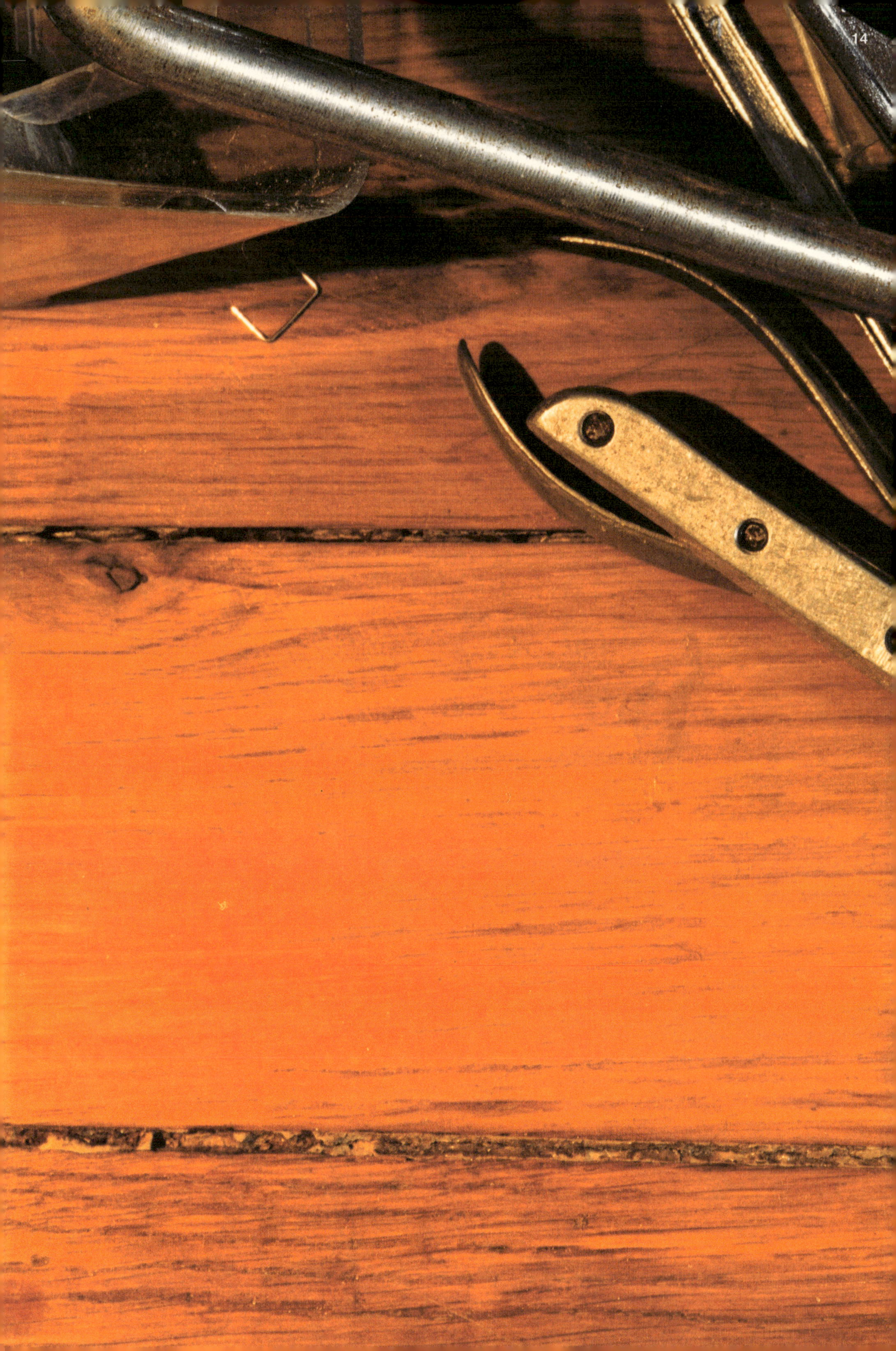

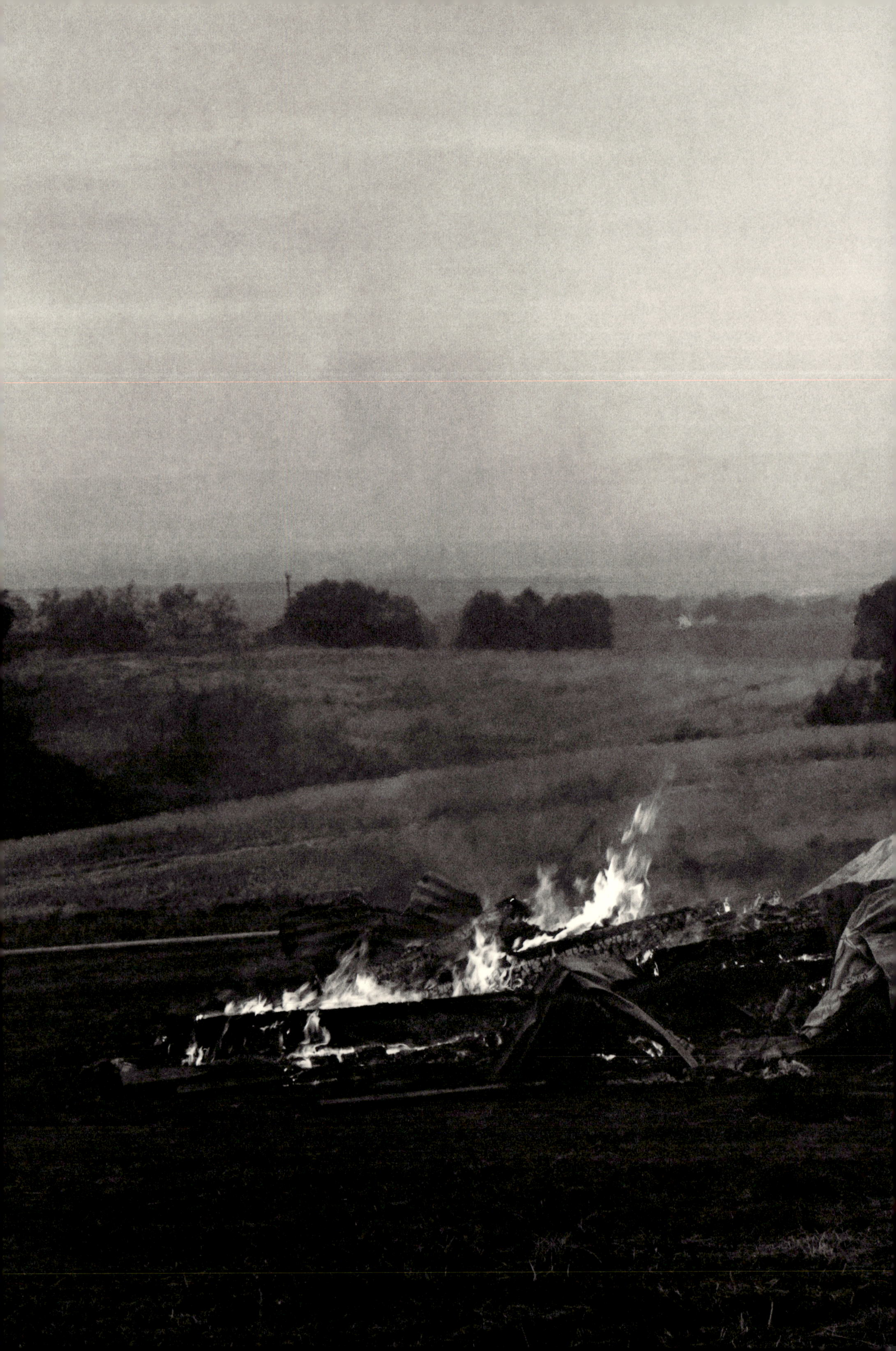

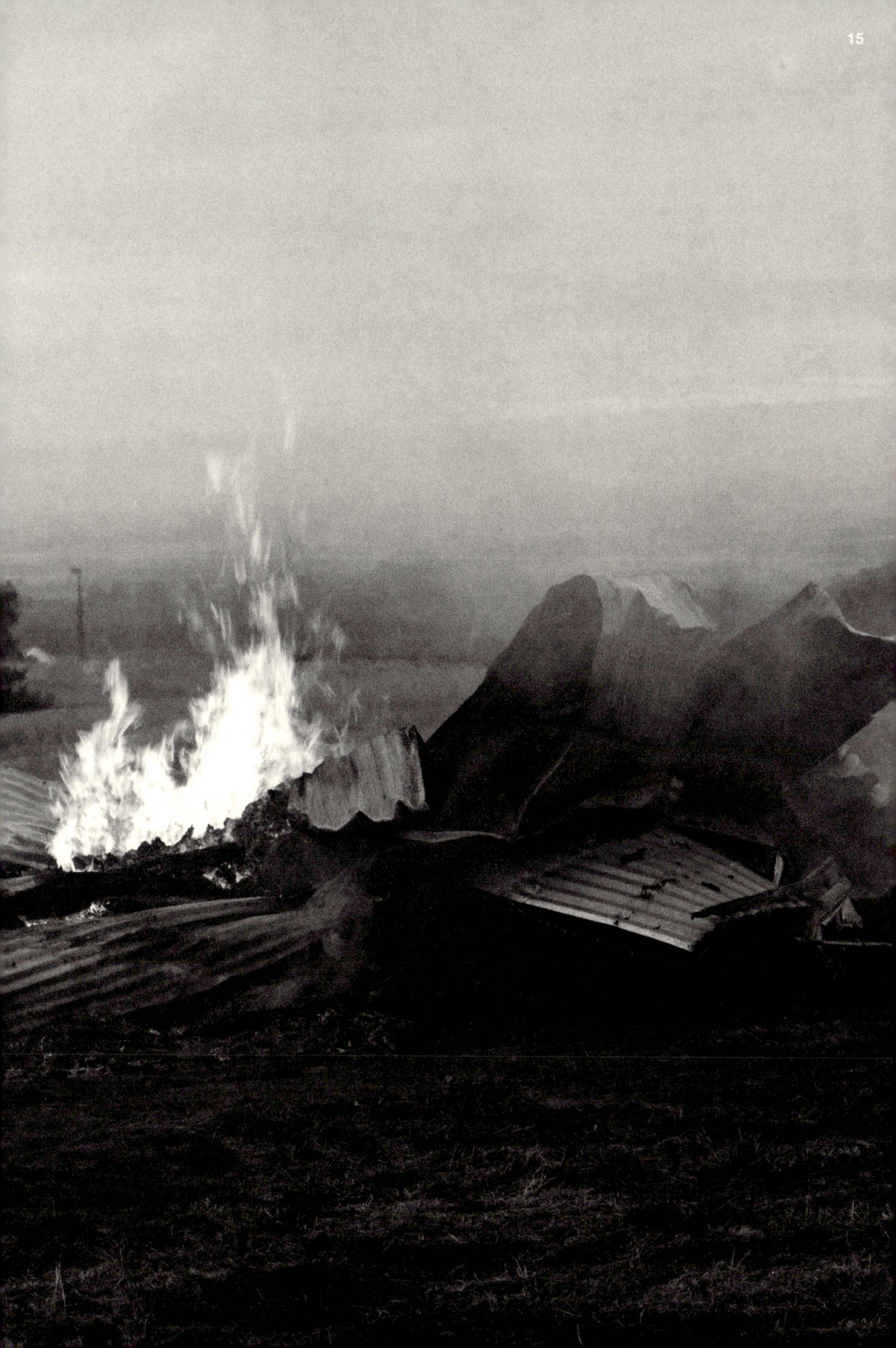

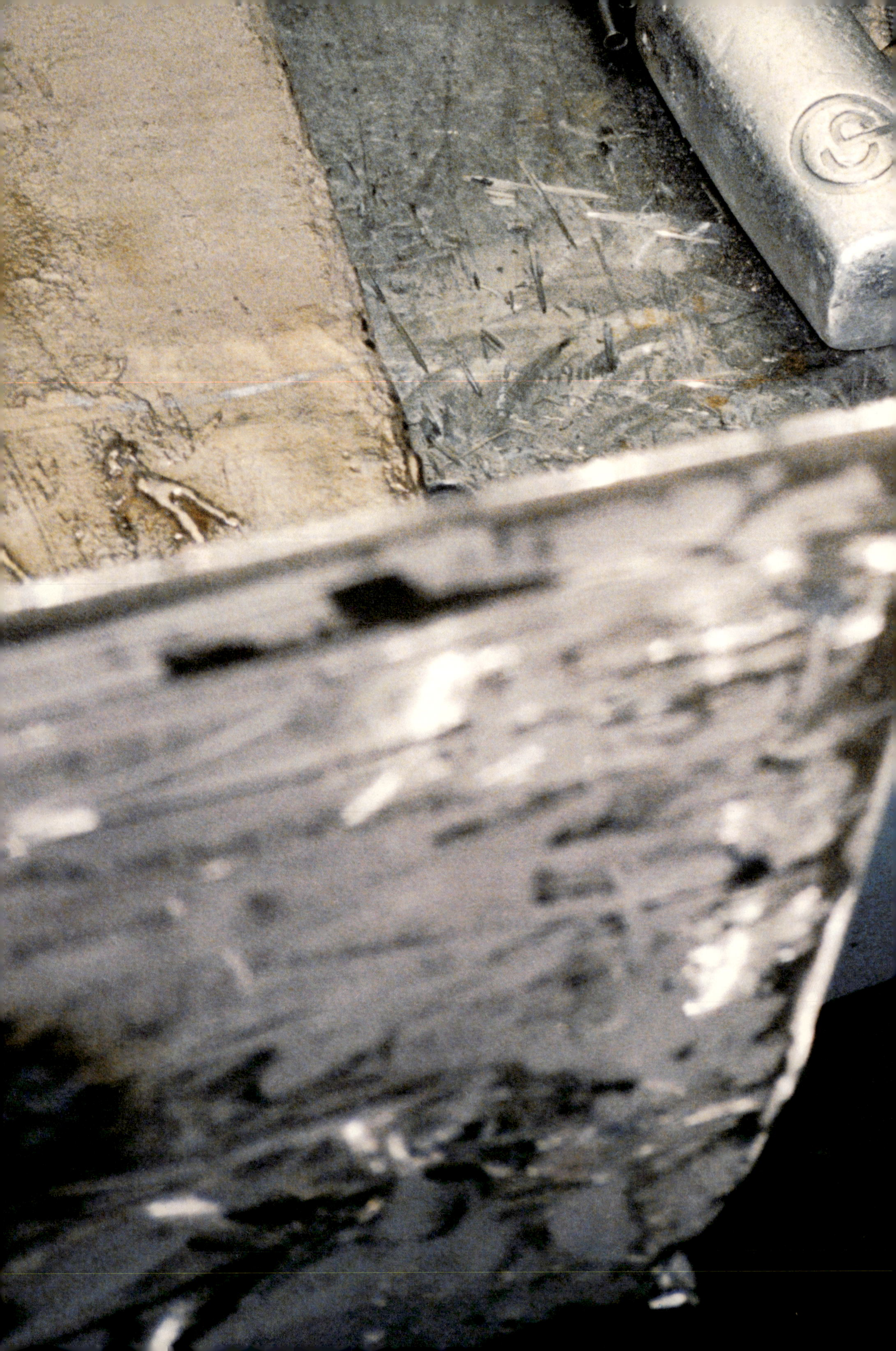

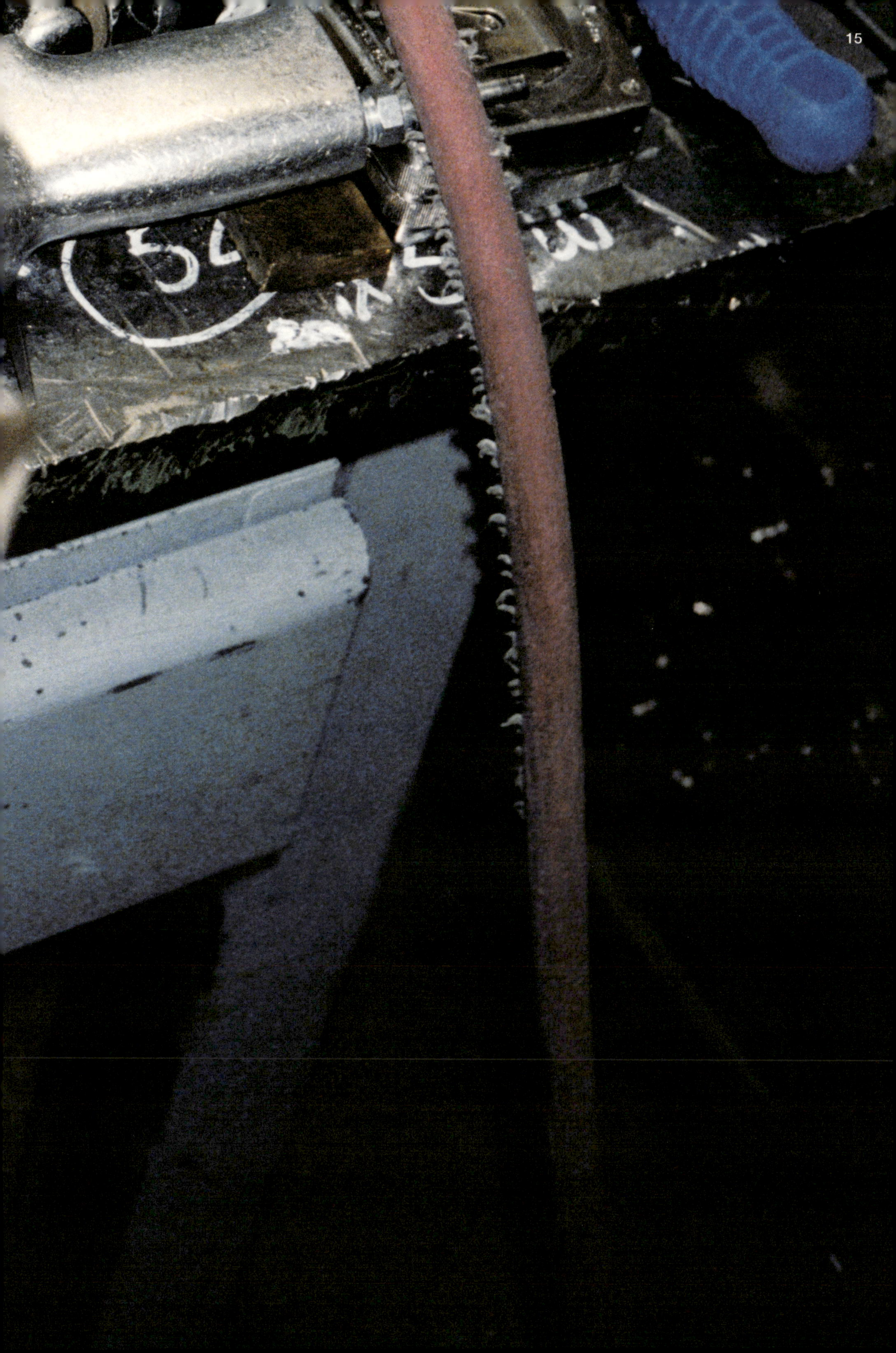

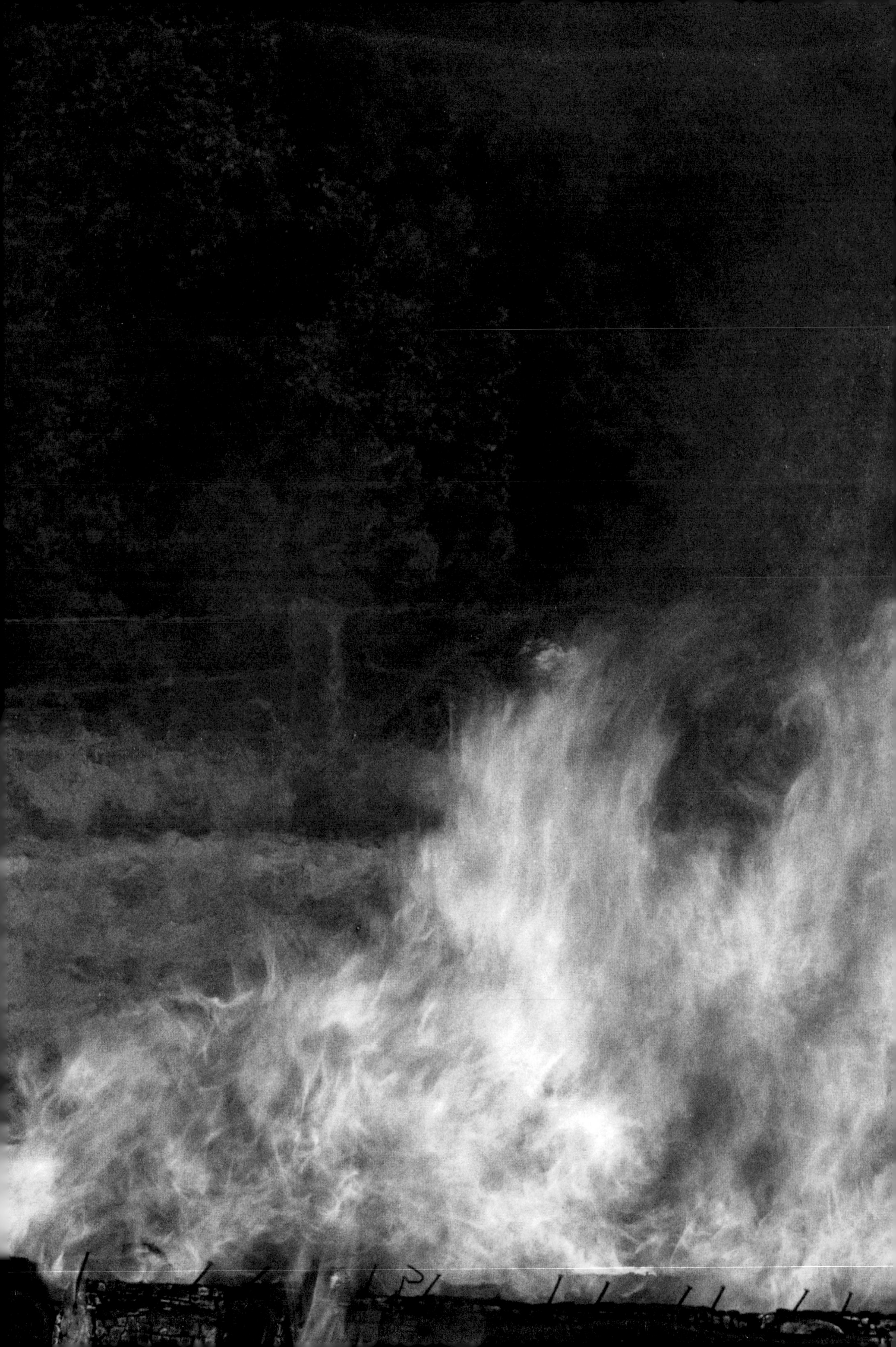

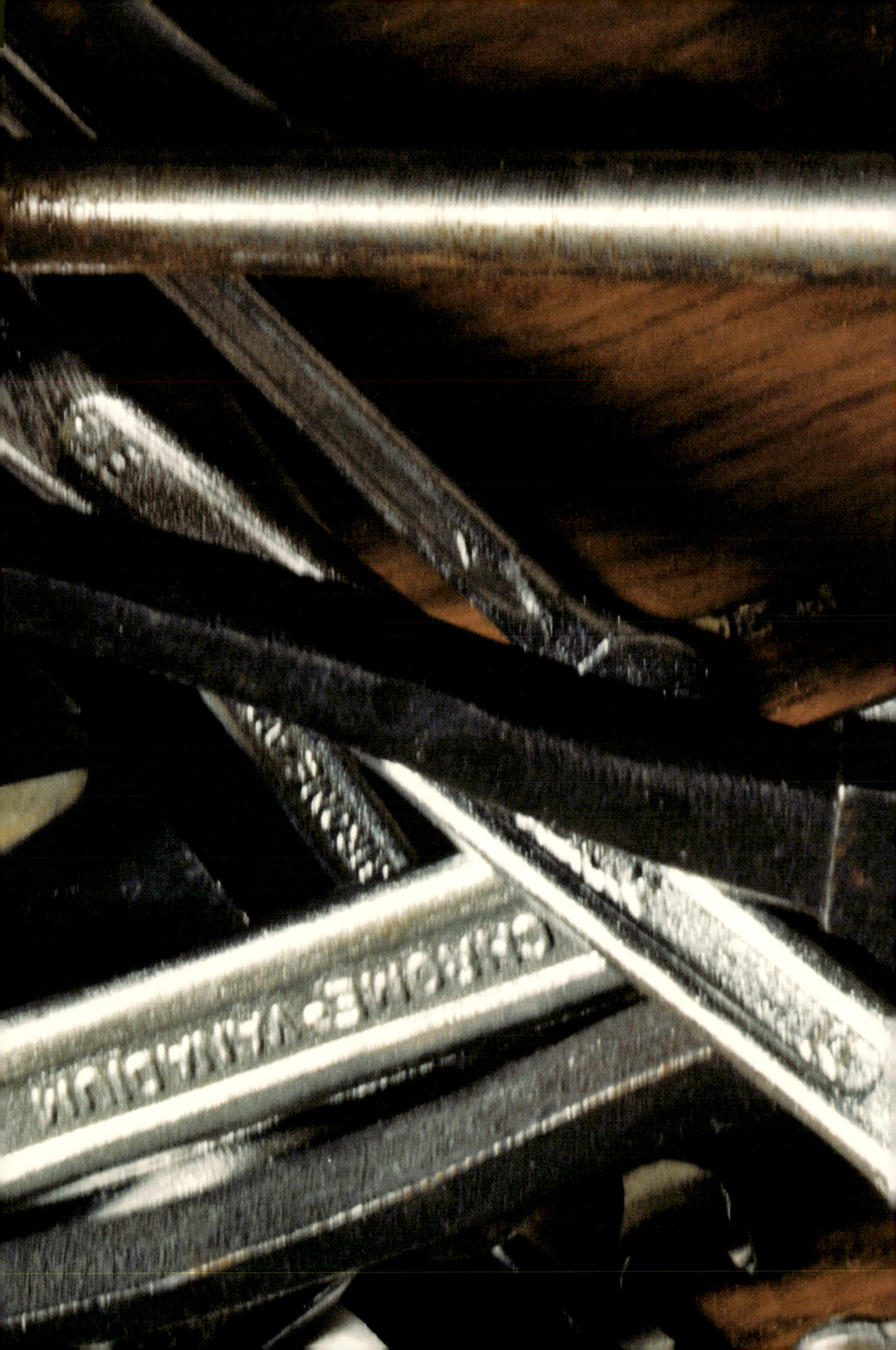
CHROME-VANADIUM

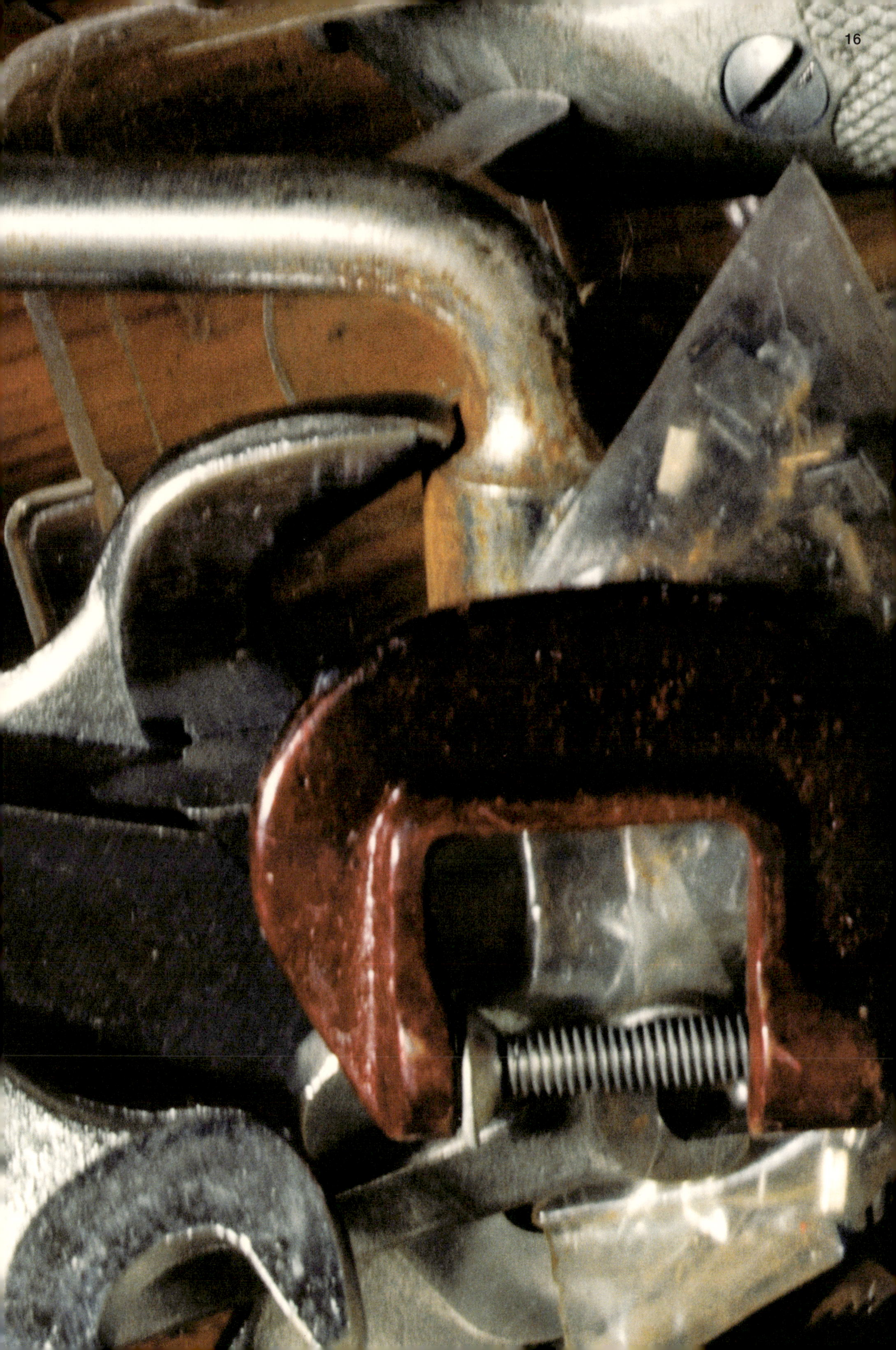

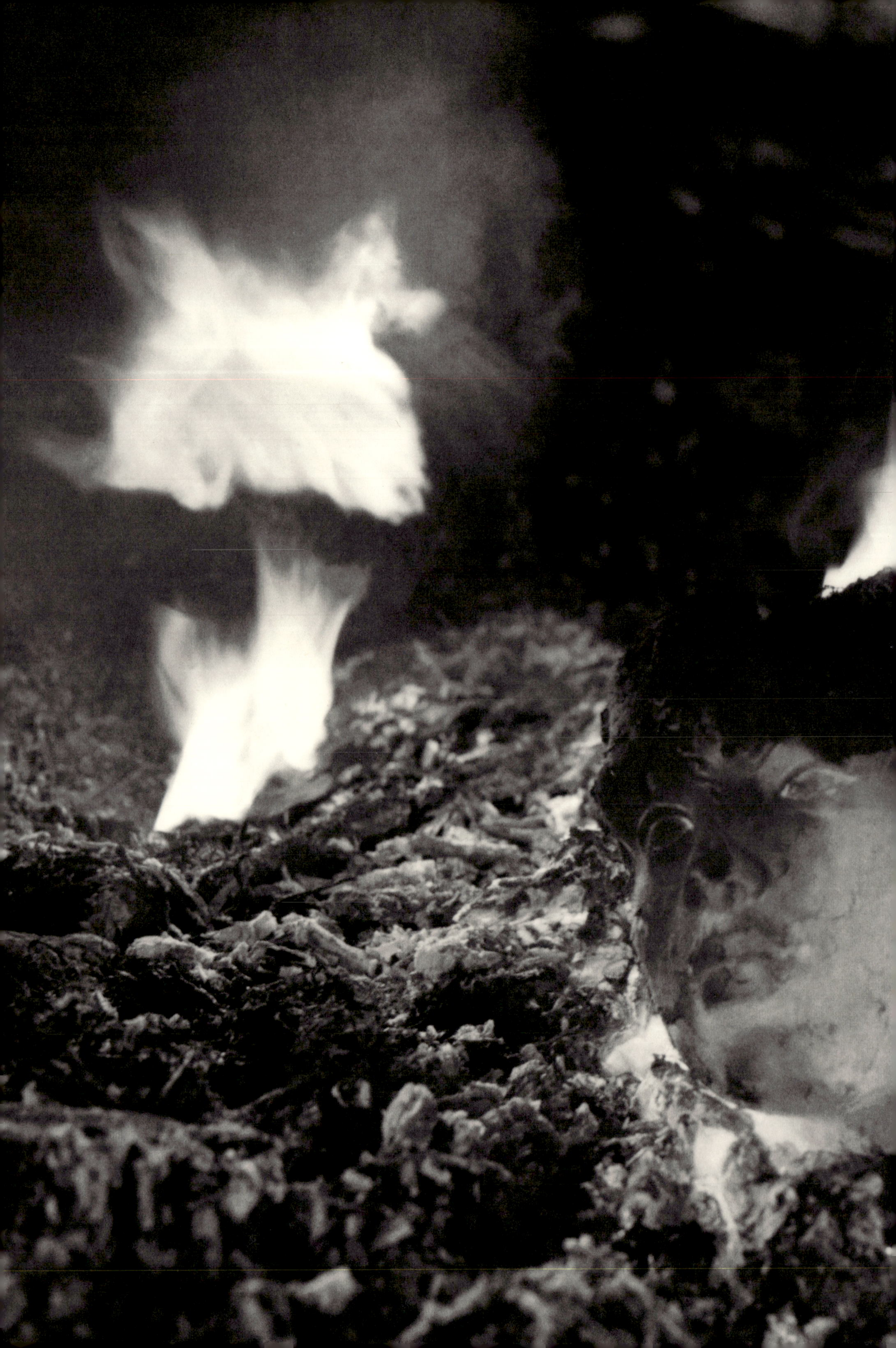

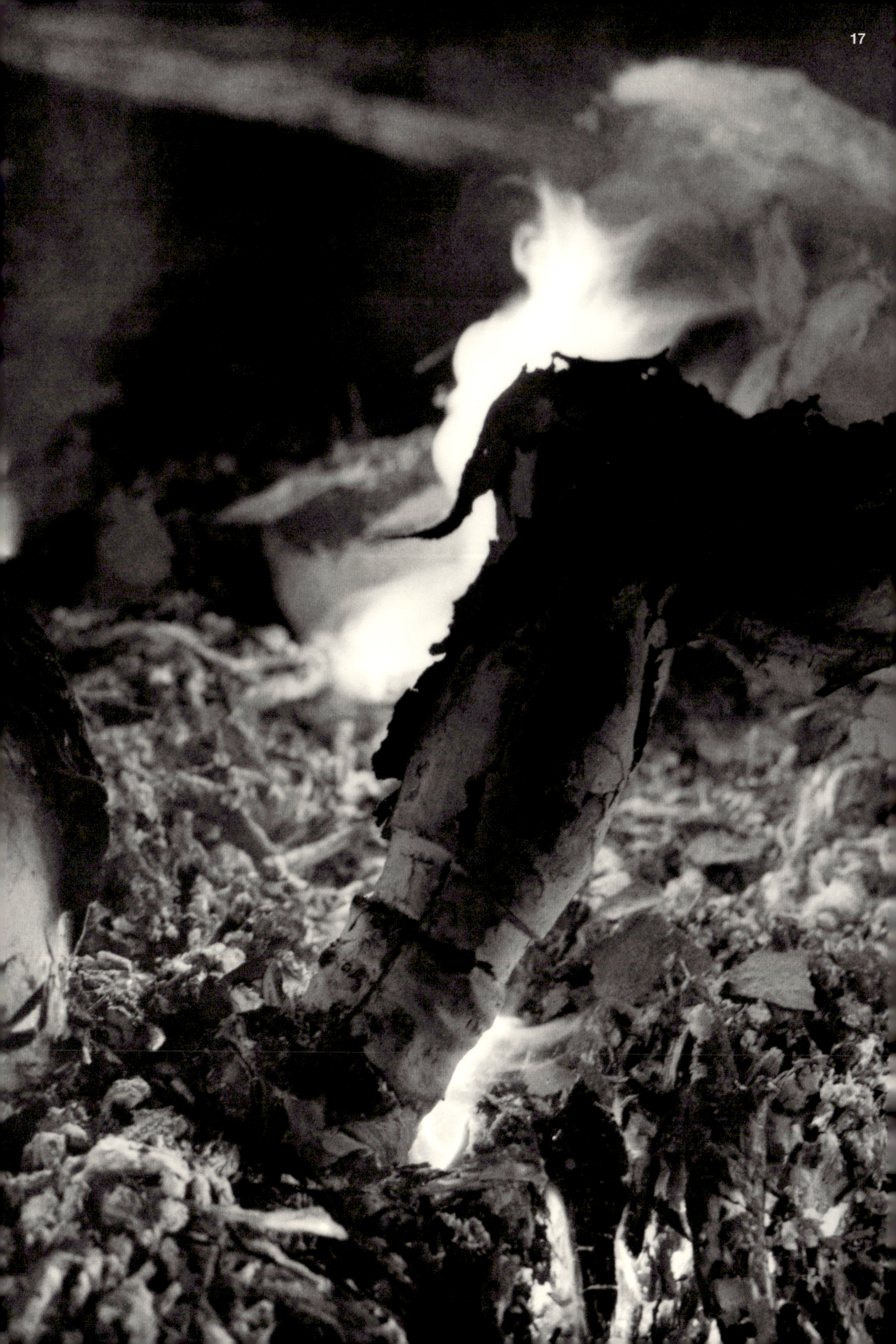

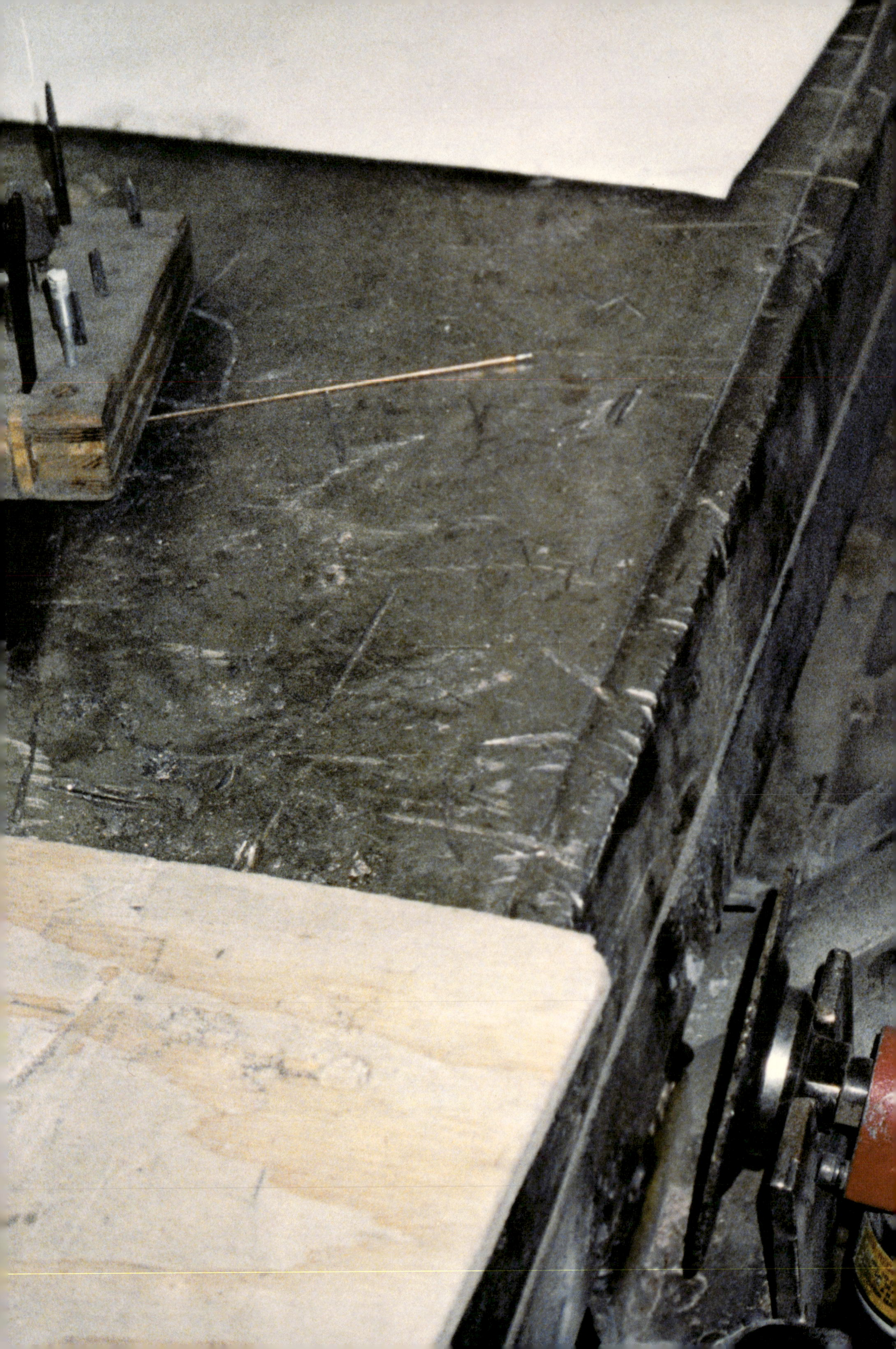

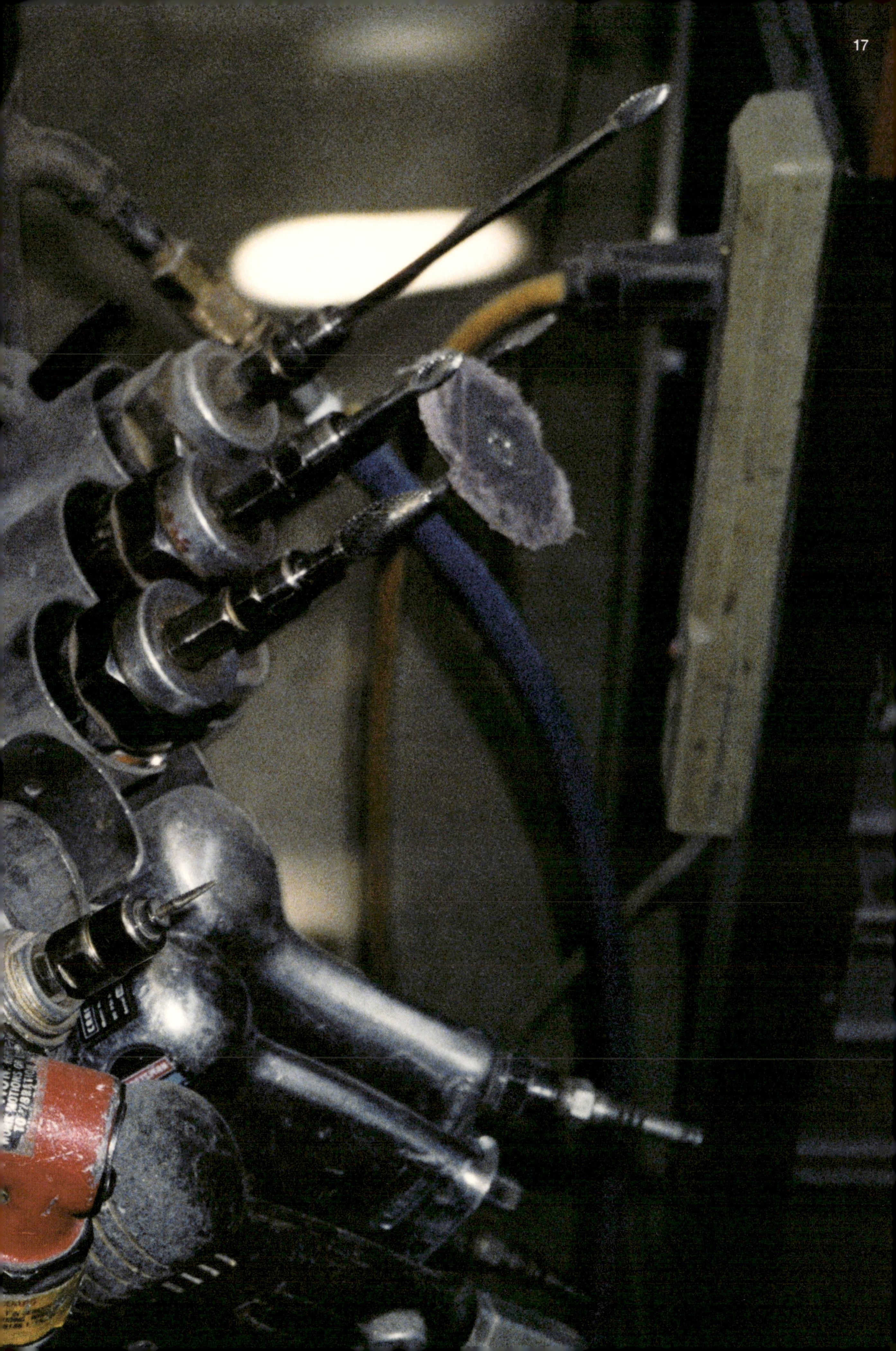

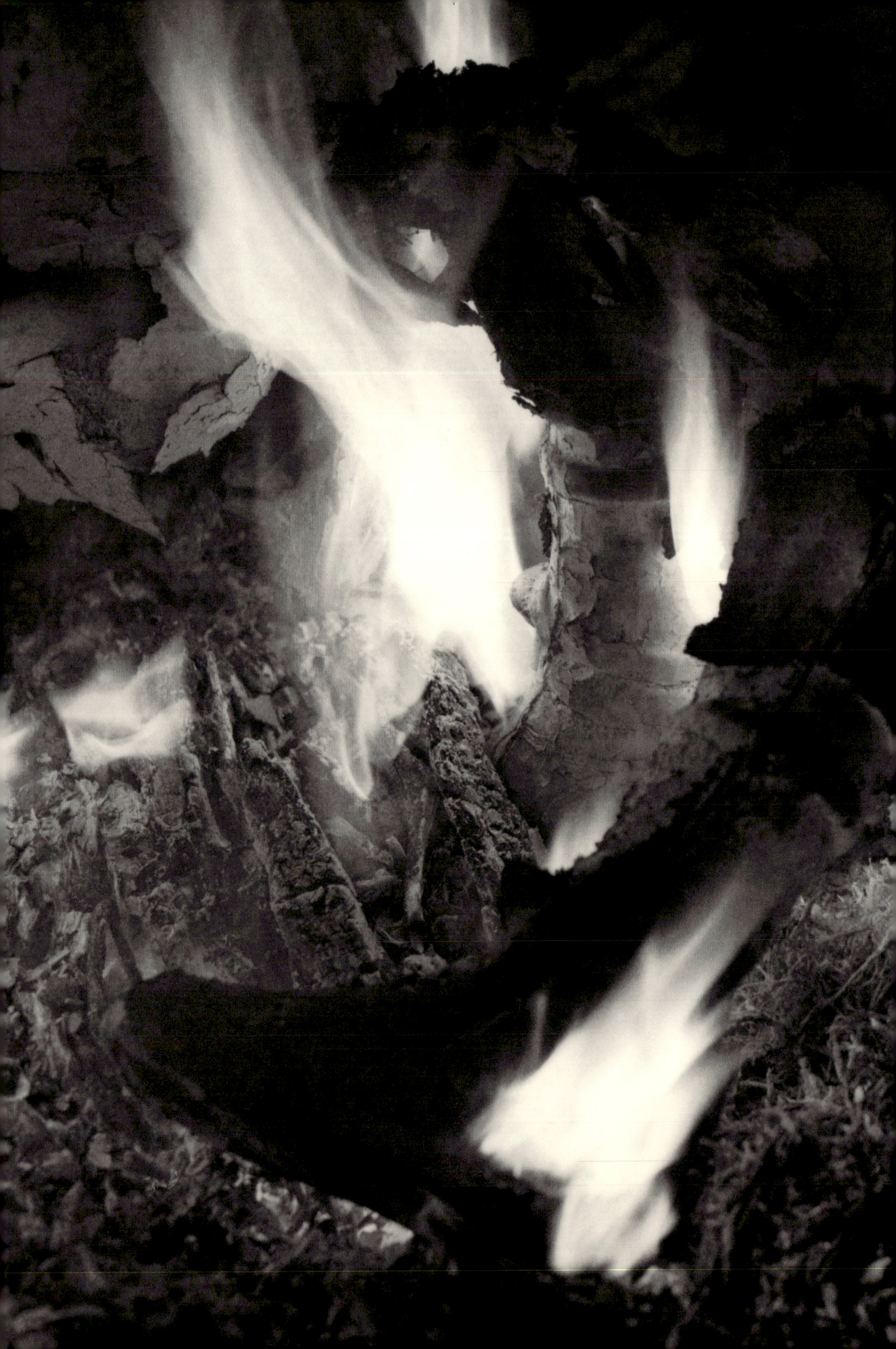

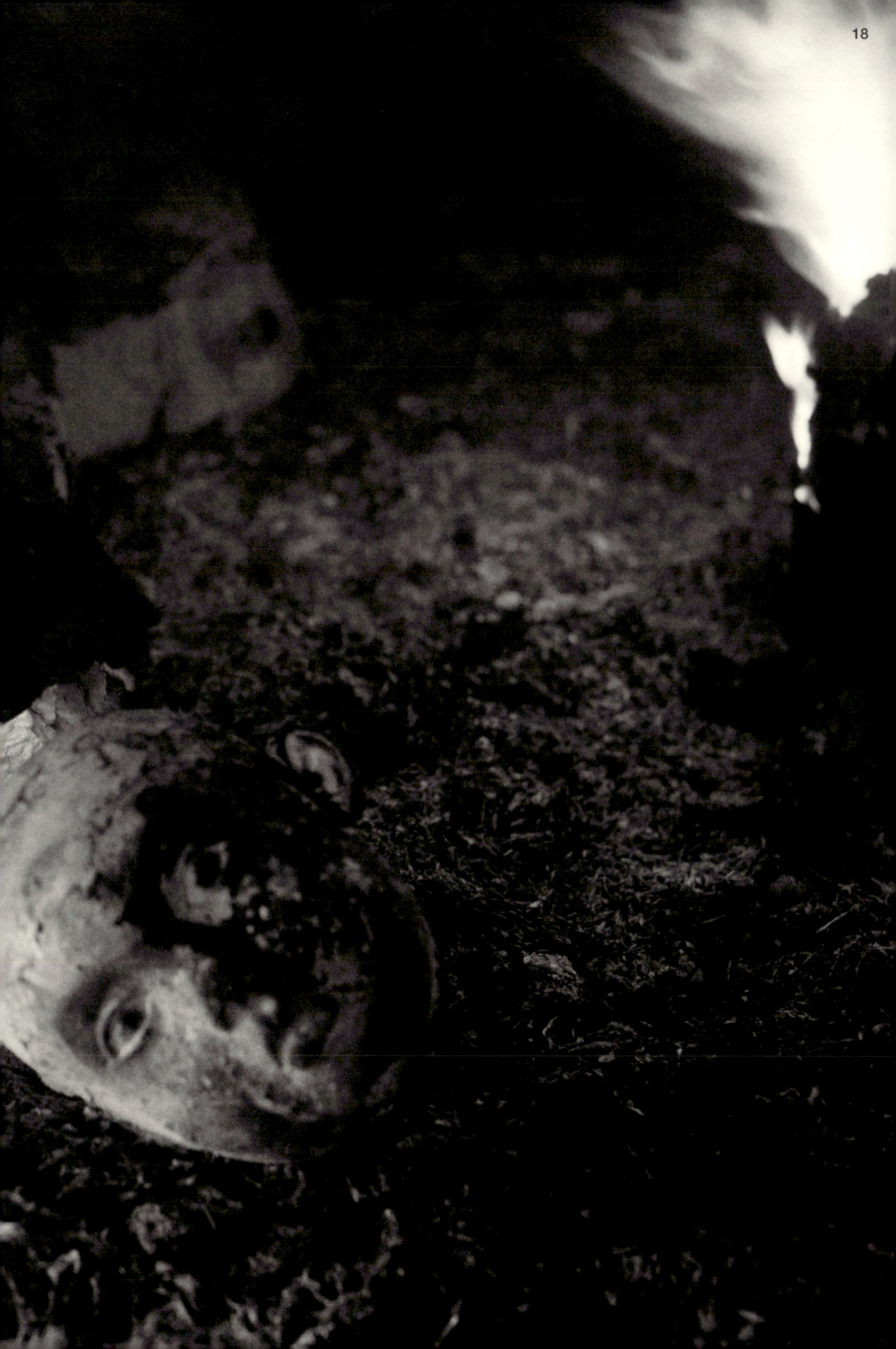

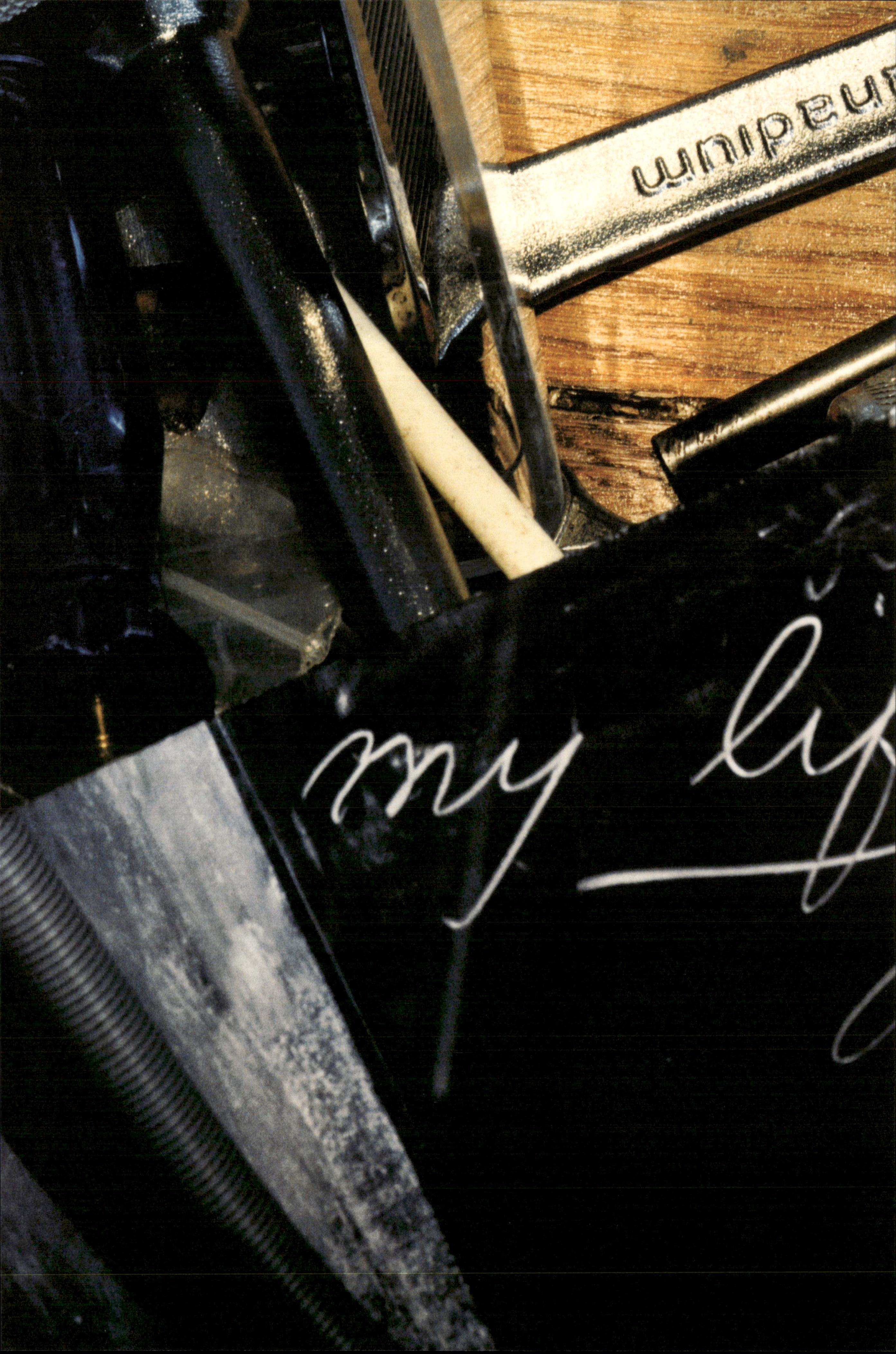
my

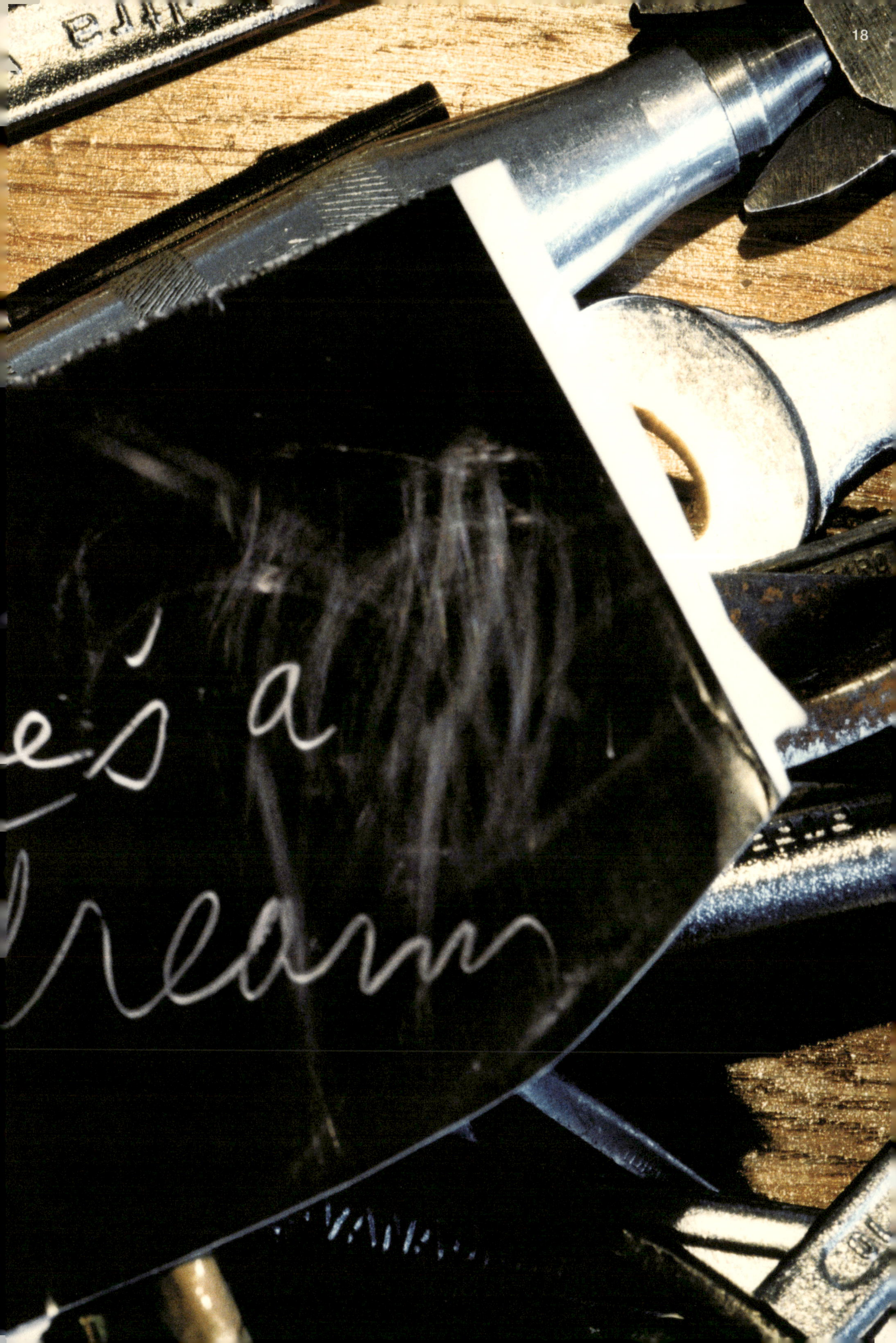

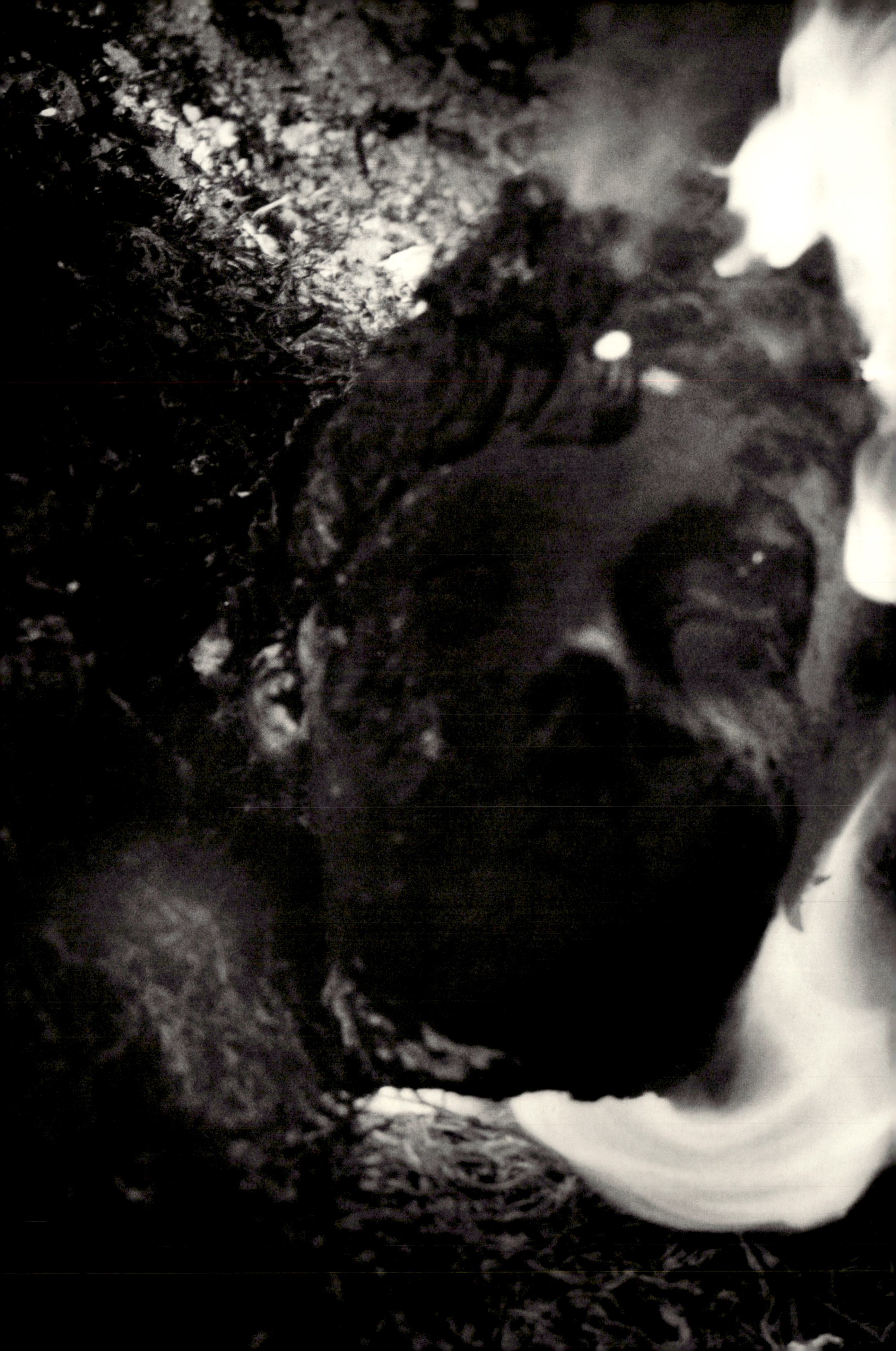

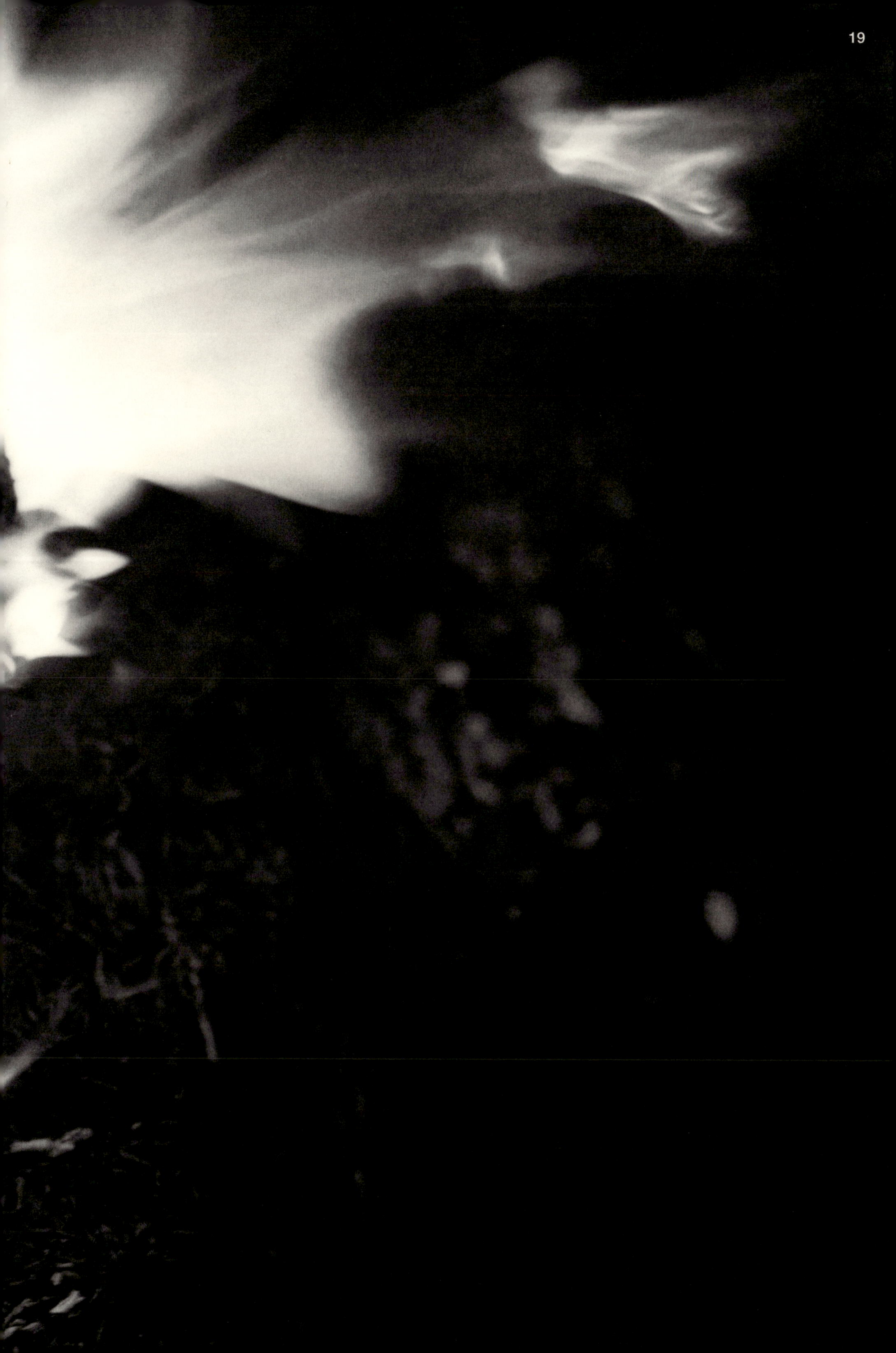

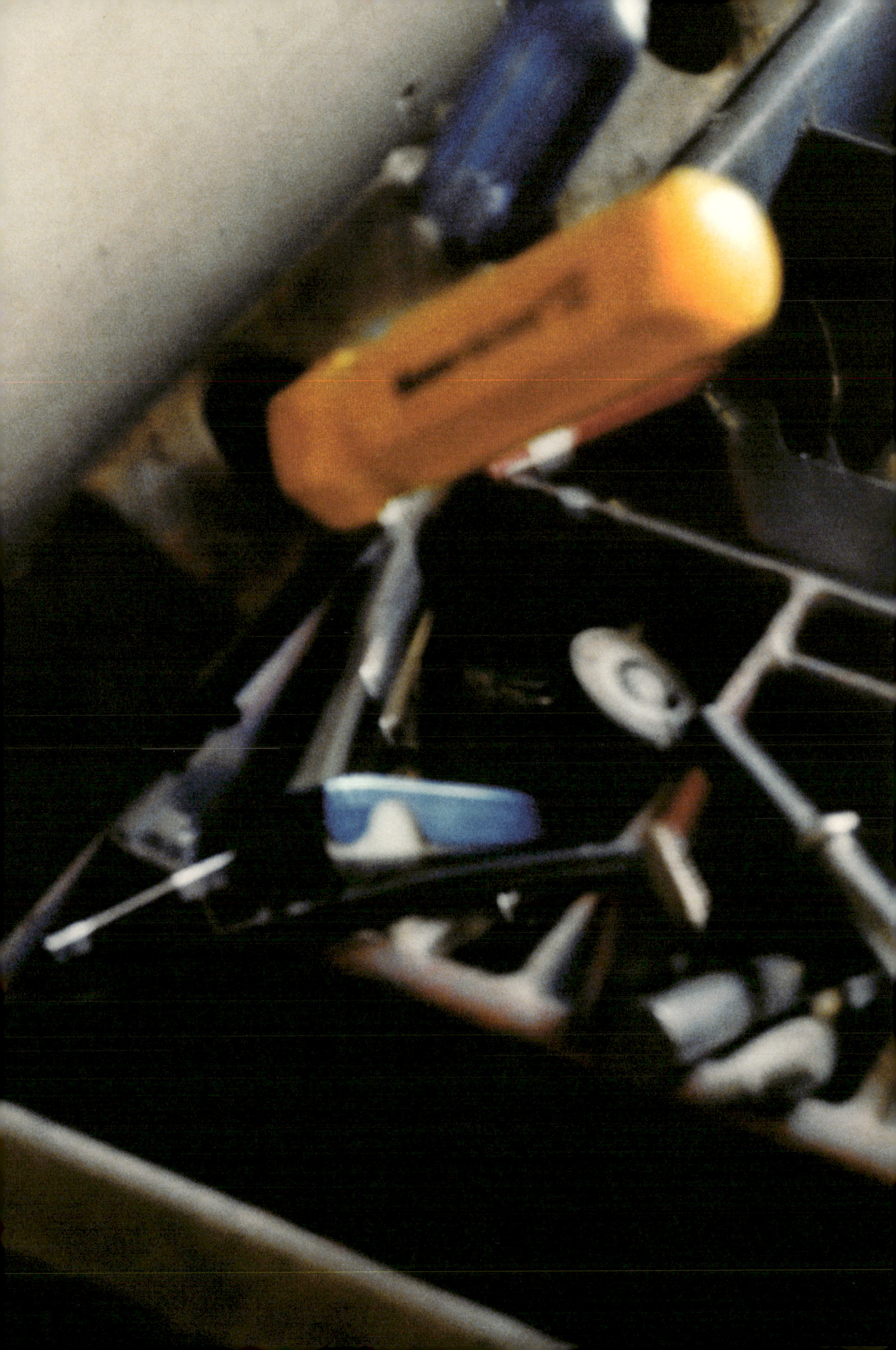

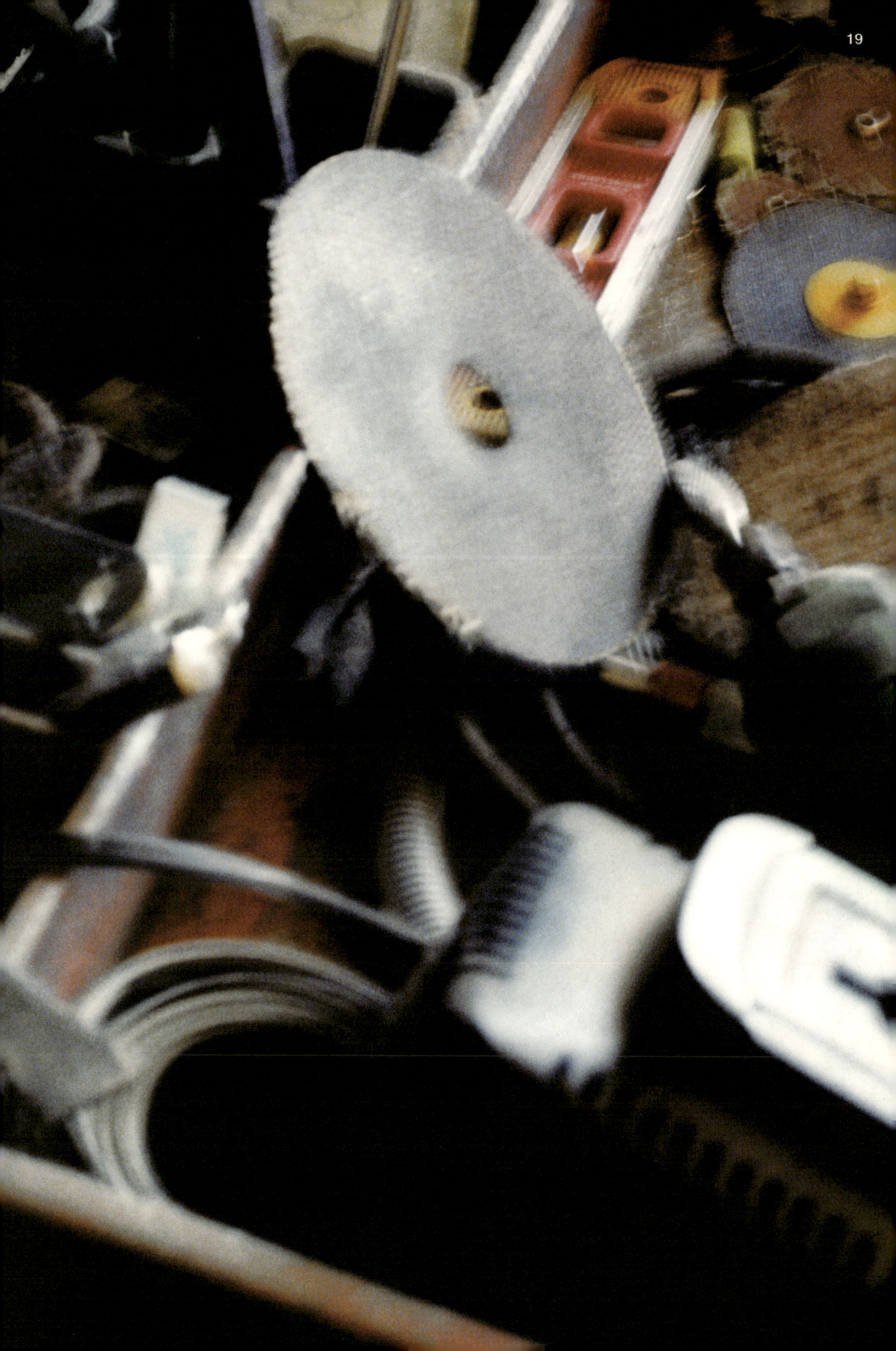

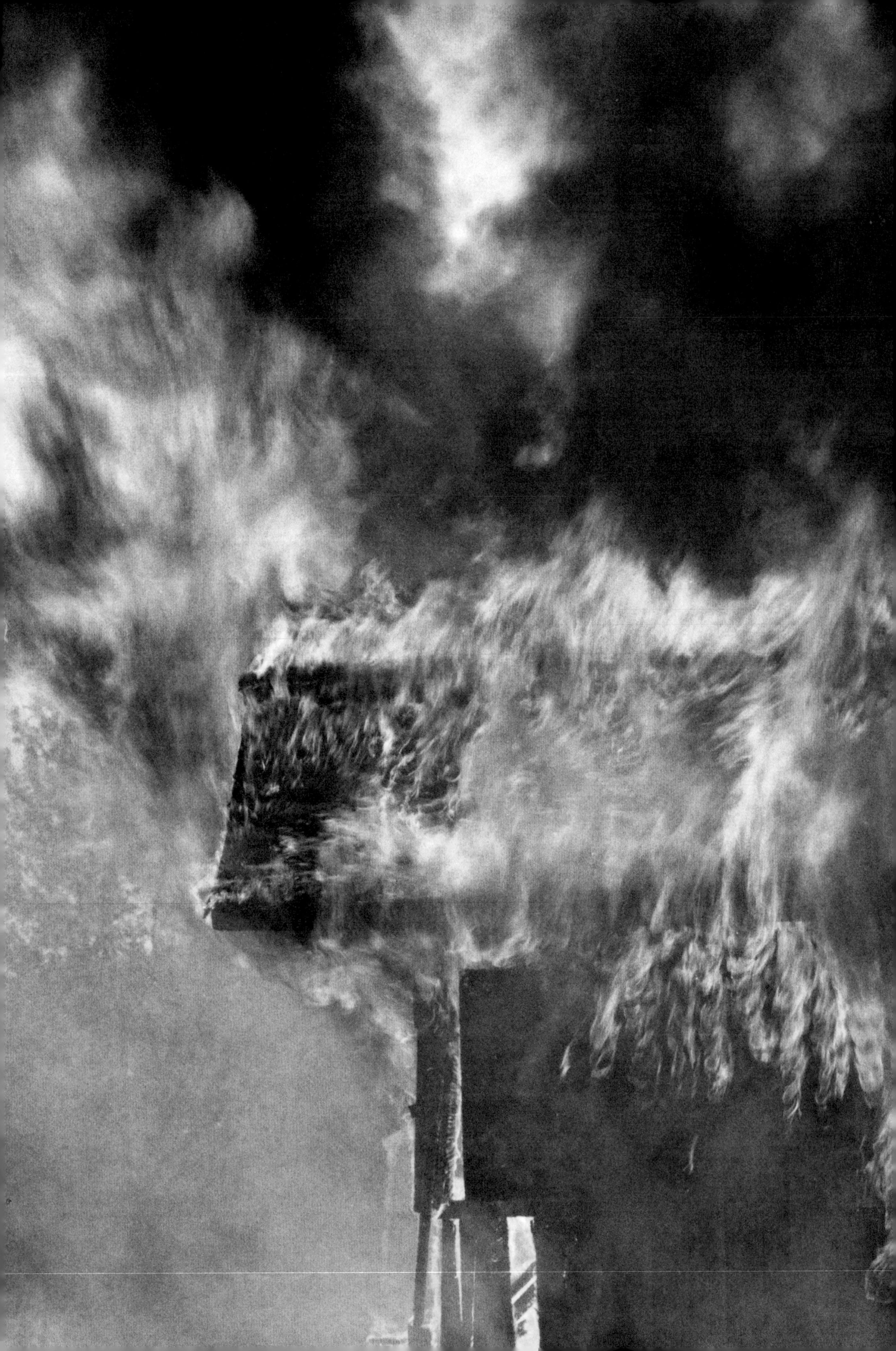

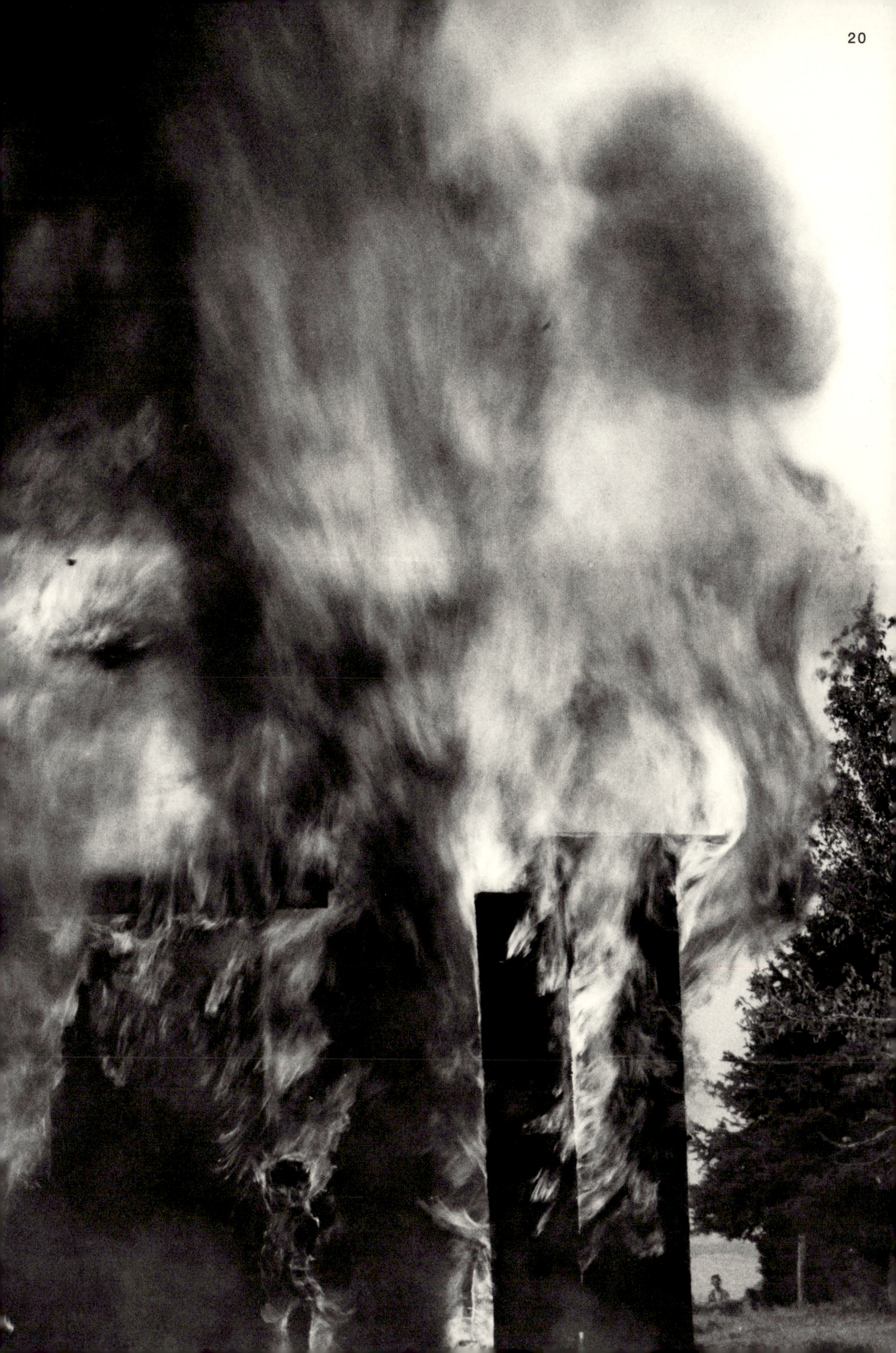

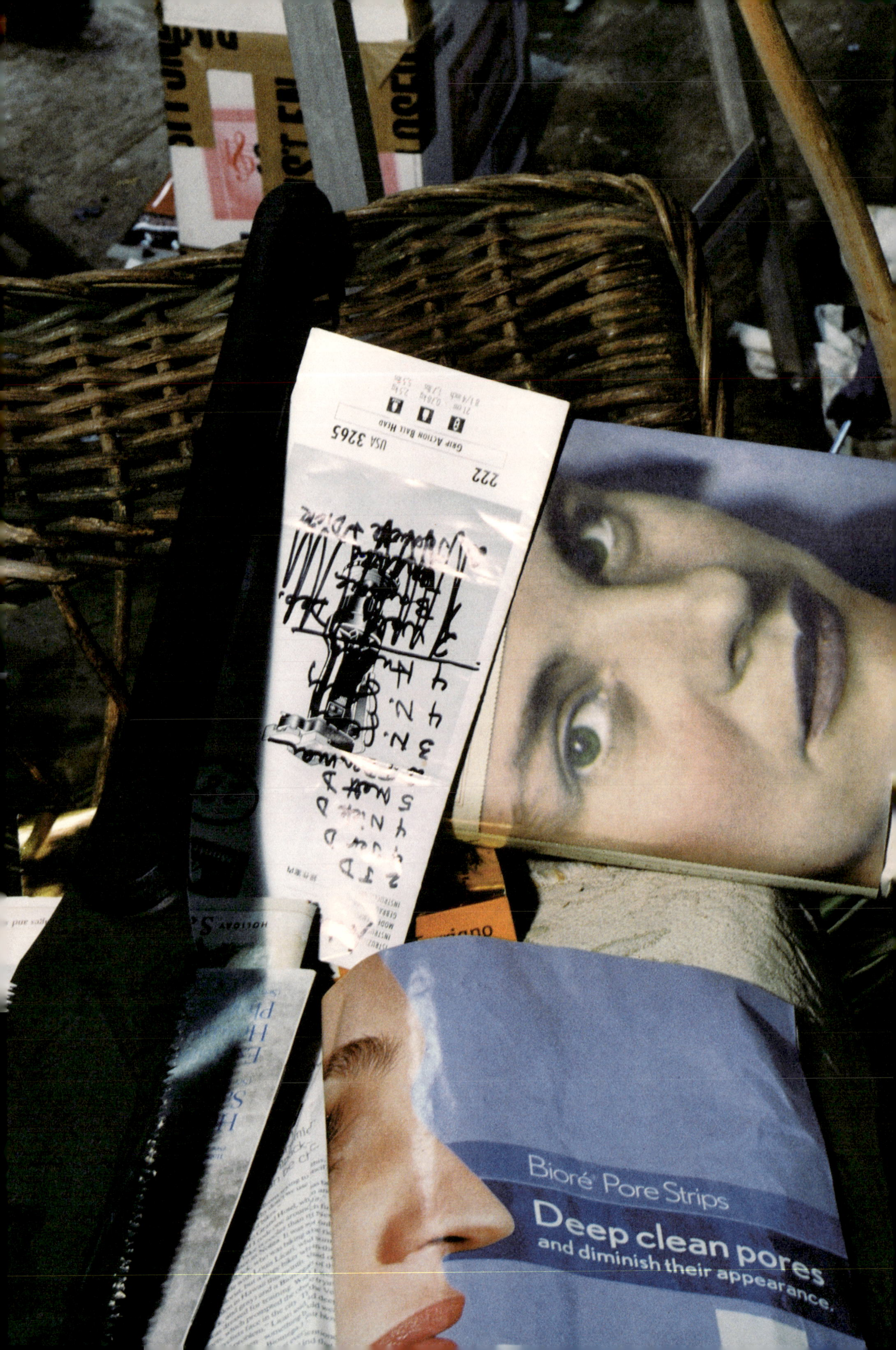
Bioré Pore Strips
Deep clean pores
and diminish their appearance.

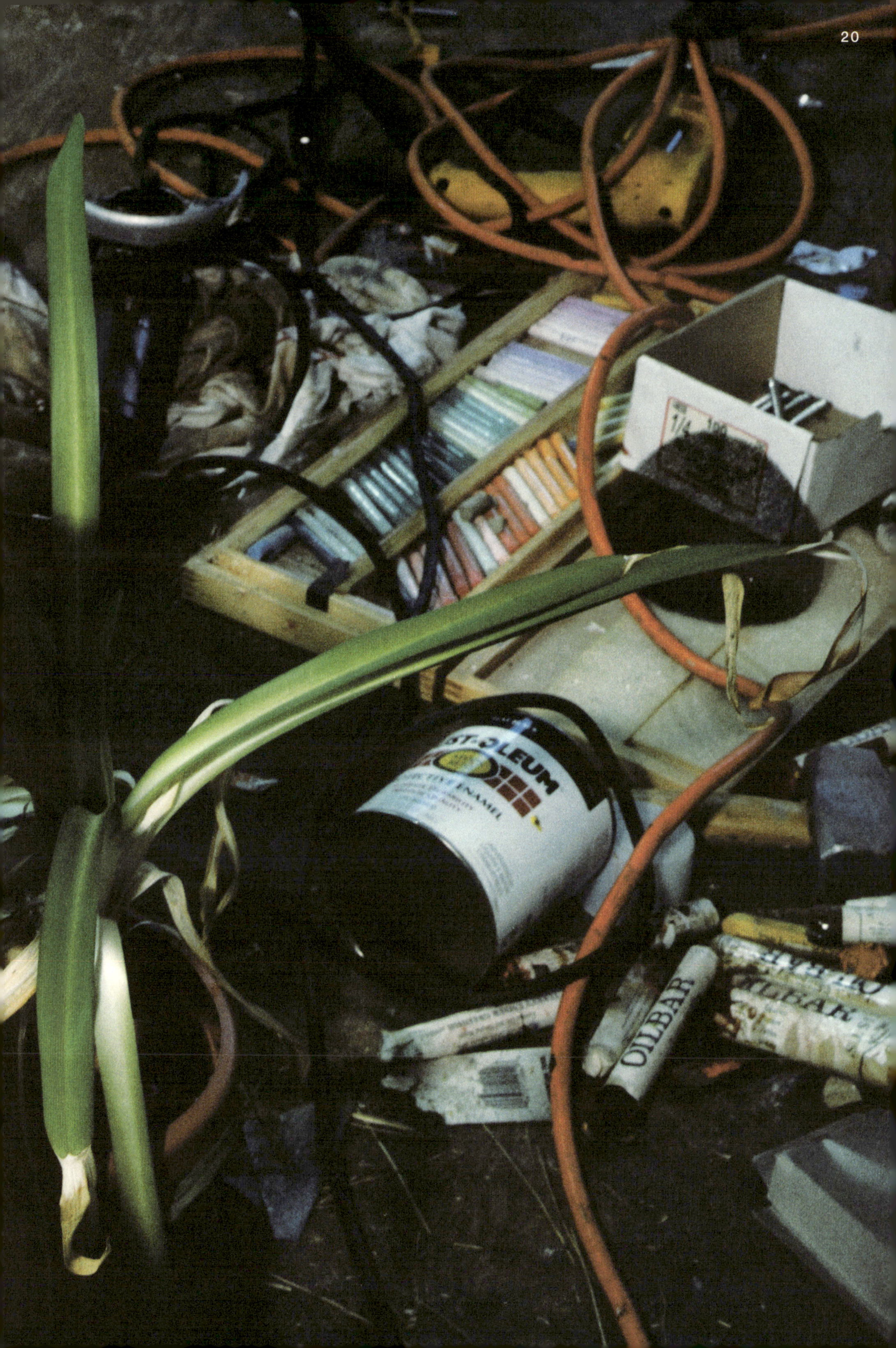
OILBAR

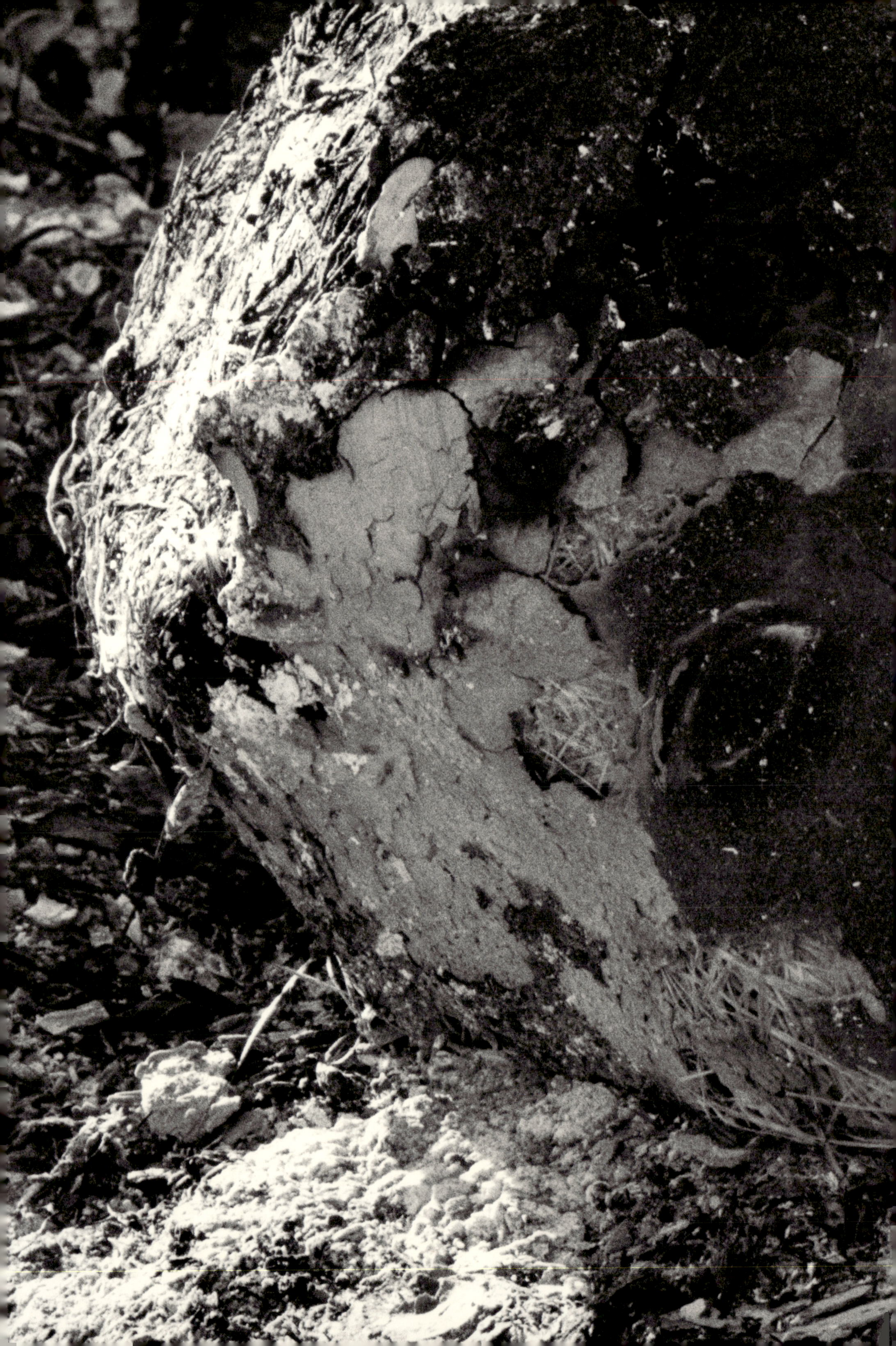

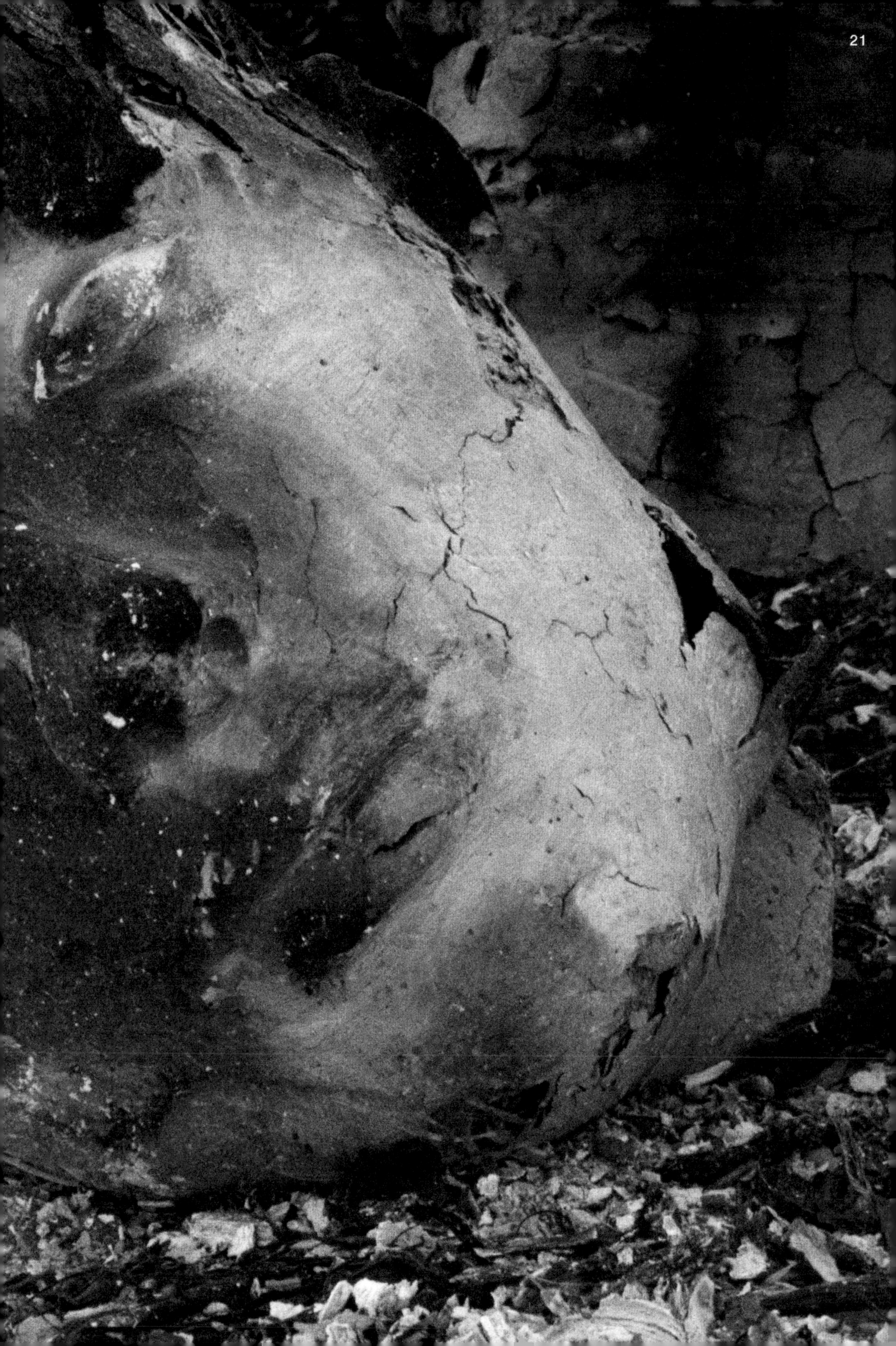

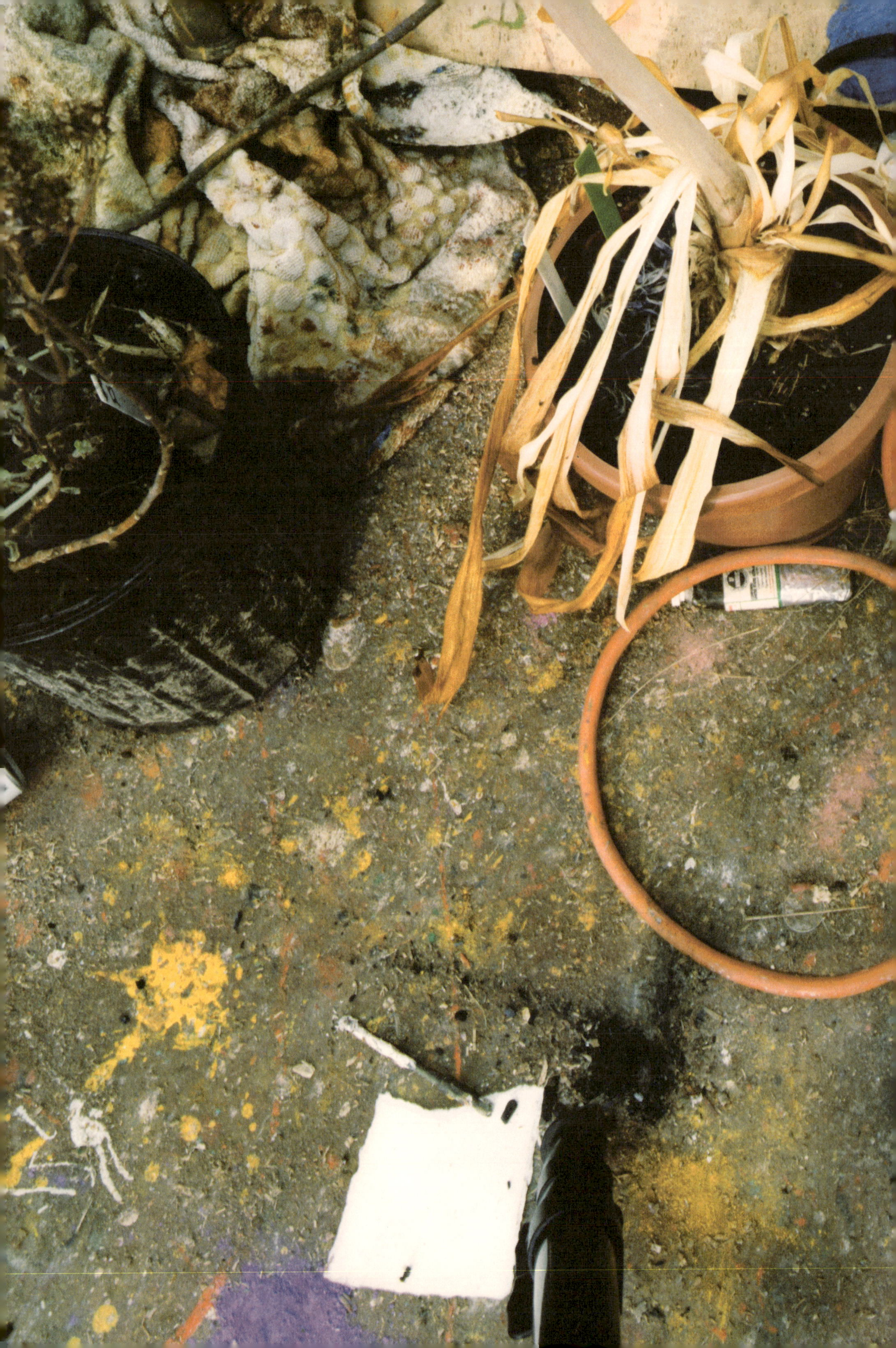

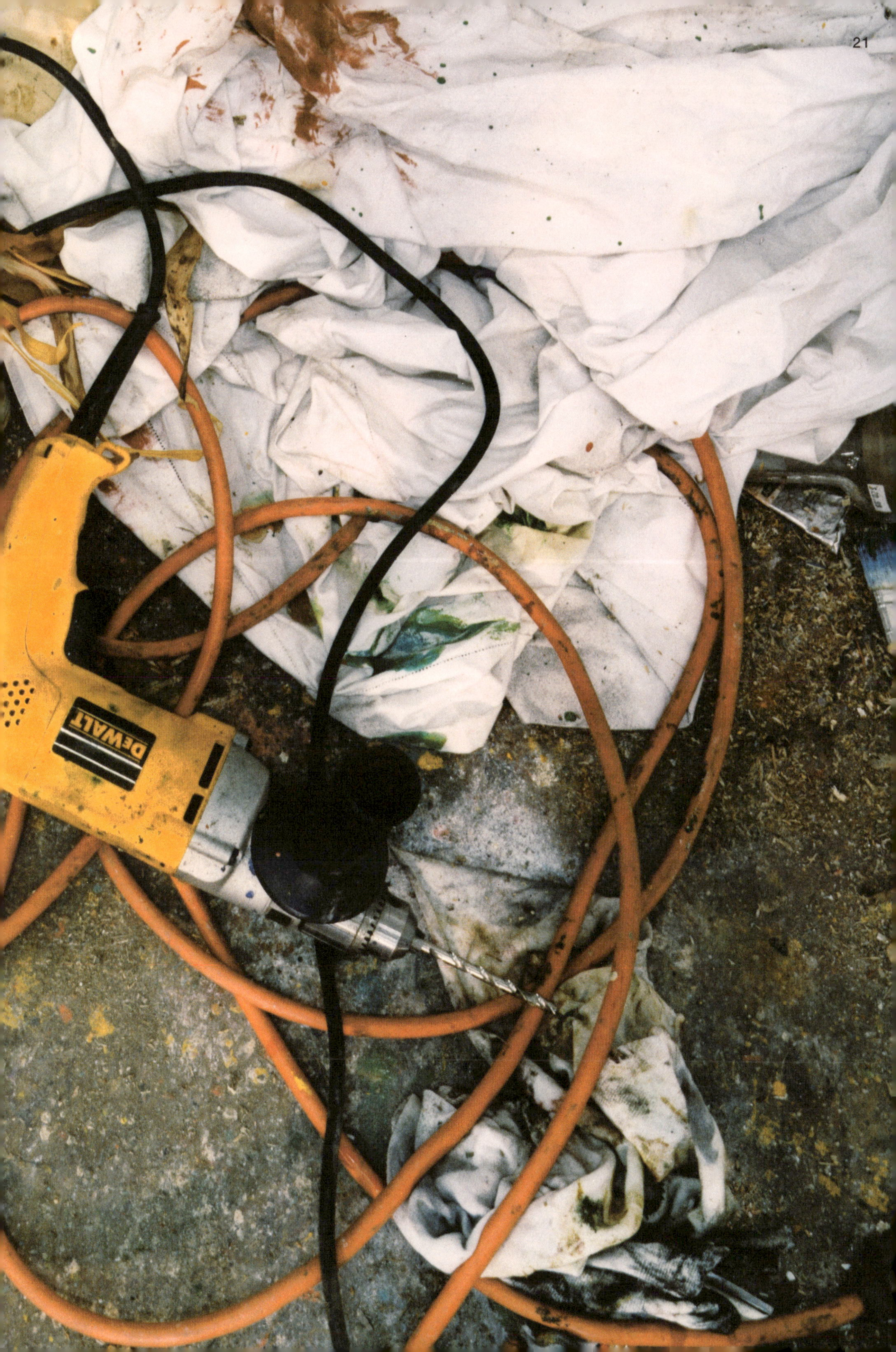
DEWALT

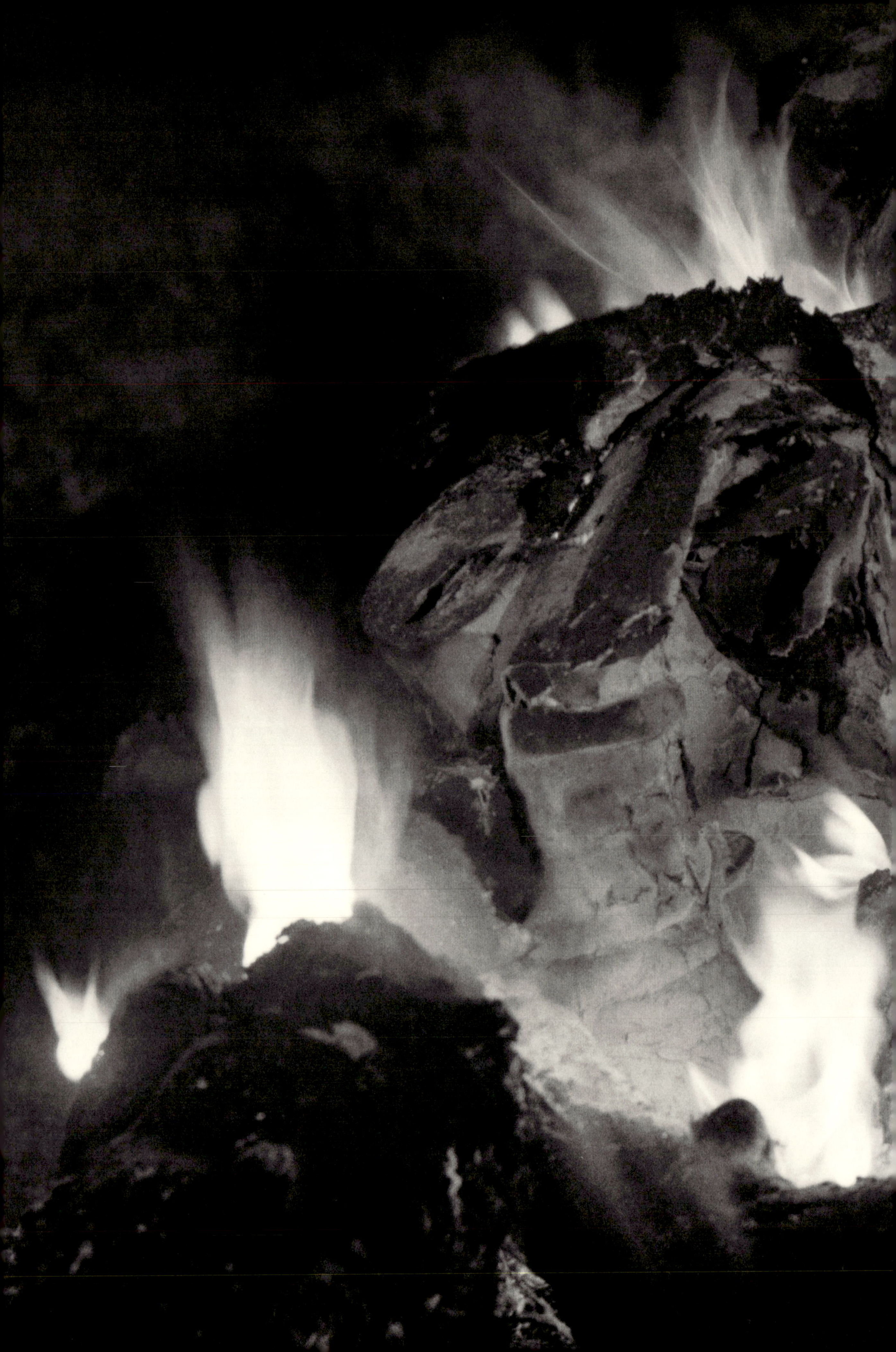

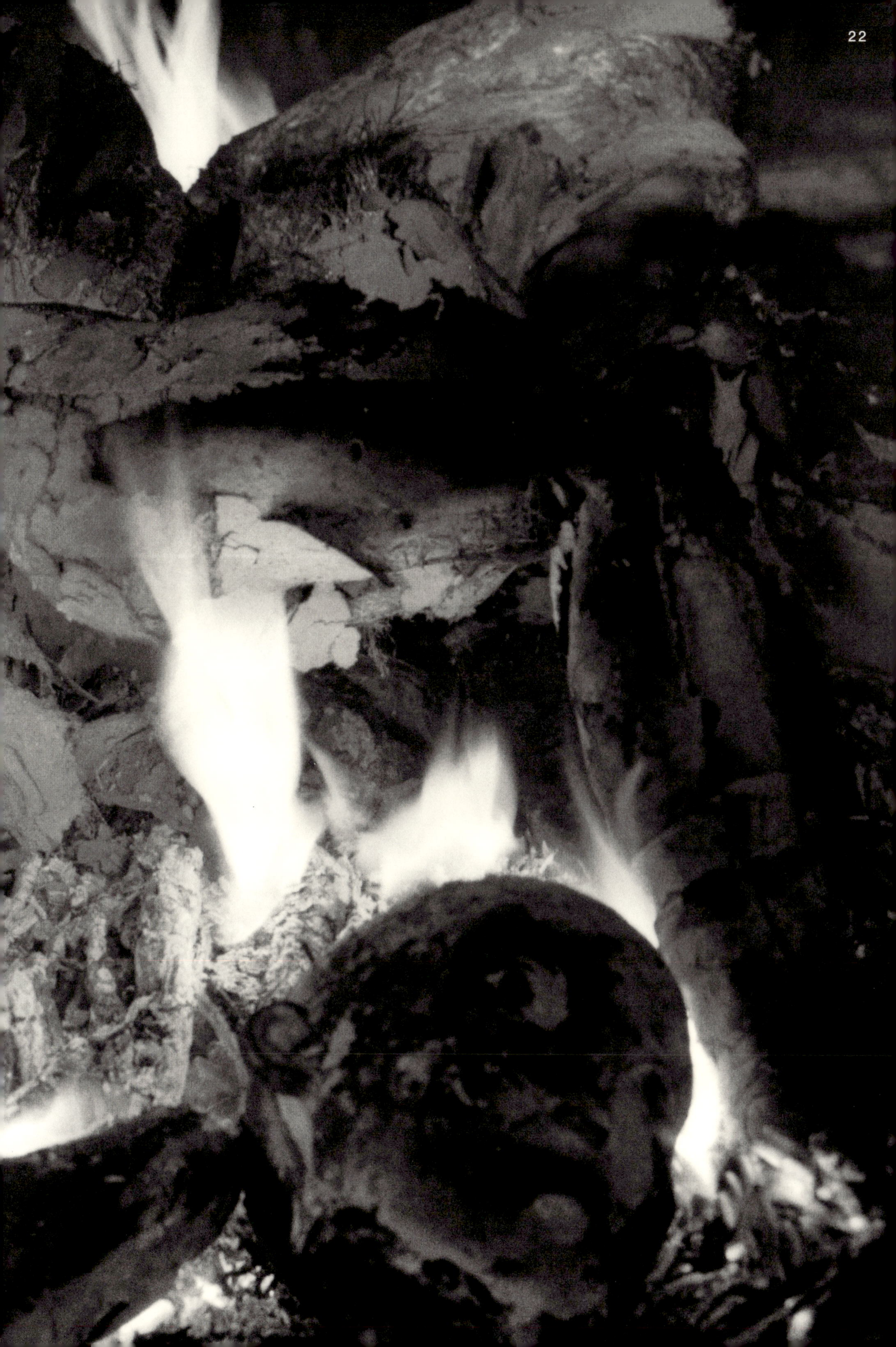

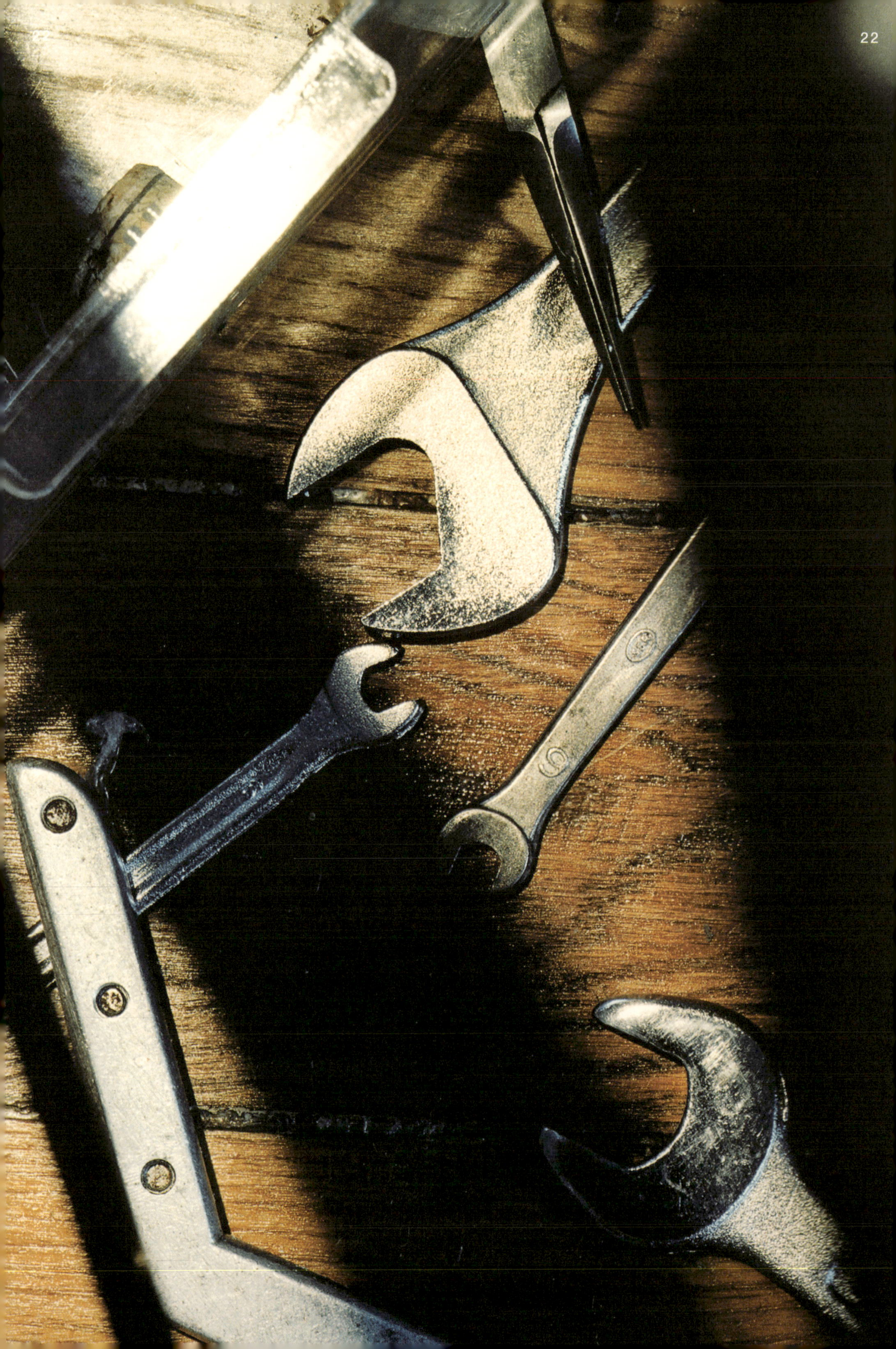

The End

Gallery Nature Morte, New Delhi,
and Bose Pacia Gallery, New York

present new photography by
Jim Dine and *Diana Michener*

December 28, 2005 – January 10, 2006
A–1 Neeti Bagh, New Delhi 110 017, India

GALLERY NATURE MORTE

A–1 Neeti Bagh, New Delhi
110 017 India

BOSE PACIA GALLERY

508 W 26th Street
New York, N.Y. 10001

Diana Michener

List of Plates

Diana Michener is represented by Pace McGill Gallery, New York

Jim Dine

List of Plates

Jim Dine is represented by PaceWildenstein, New York

First edition 2006

Book design: Diana Michener, Jim Dine, Gerhard Steidl
Scans done at Steidl's digital darkroom
Production and printing:
Steidl / Düstere Str. 4 / D–37073 Göttingen
Phone +49 551-49 60 60 / Fax +49 551-49 60 649
E-mail: mail@steidl.de
www.steidlville.com / www.steidl.de

ISBN 3-86521-259-X
ISBN 13 978-3-86521-259-7
Printed in Germany